CONTENTS

CONTENTS

CONTENTS

TABLE OF CASES

TABLE OF STATUTES

CHAPTER 1

INTRODUCTION

1 THE ORIGINS OF SALES LAW

This book gives an account of the law which governs the various **1-01**
ways in which goods may be supplied. It is worth spending a moment
to explain where this law comes from. Goods are usually, though not
always, supplied under a contract (see 'Non-Contractual Supply',
Chapter 2). English law has a body of rules known as 'the law of
contract' which, in principle, apply to all contracts of whatever kind.
Virtually all readers of this book will already have studied a course on
the law of contract or a course on the law of obligations of which the law
of contract was part. In addition to these rules English law has
developed rules which are peculiar to particular contracts, such as sale
of goods, hire-purchase, insurance, employment and so on.

It is often difficult to discover where the line is drawn between
general rules applicable to all contracts and specialised rules relating to
particular contracts. All the cases discussed in accounts of the general
law of contract necessarily relate to special kinds of contract. Many of
these cases will involve sales of goods but a good many will be treated
as laying down rules for all types of contract and not simply for
contracts of sale of goods.

Another problem arises from the fact that, whereas the law of
contract consists of principles which have to be culled from thousands
of cases (with a few relatively minor statutory changes), the law of sale
of goods is, exceptionally for English law, to be found in a single
statutory code. In 1893 Parliament passed the Sale of Goods Act. This
Act was designed to *codify* the common law on sale of goods, that is, to
state the effect of the decisions of the courts in a succinct statutory form.
The draftsman of the Act, Sir MacKenzie Chalmers, was not trying to
change the law but to state it clearly and accurately though it does
appear that in a few cases he anticipated developments which the courts
had not yet made.

Judges have repeatedly said that in deciding the meaning of a **1-02**
codifying statute like the Sale of Goods Act 1893 the cases on which it
was based should not normally be consulted. The most famous
statement is that of Lord Herschell in *Bank of England v. Vagliano Brothers*

(1891)[1] (a case decided in reference to the Bills of Exchange Act 1882, another codifying statute) where he said that:

> '... the purpose of such a statute surely was that on any point specifically dealt with by it, the law should be ascertained by interpreting the language used instead of, as before, by roaming over a vast number of authorities in order to discover what the law was, extracting it by a minute critical examination of the prior decisions.'

So, as a rule, reference to pre-1893 cases should not be necessary but there have been many cases since then and now it is often only possible to discover the accepted meaning of sections in the 1893 Act by careful examination of those cases. In addition, the 1893 Act was amended a number of times and in 1979 parliament passed a new Sale of Goods Act. This was a *consolidating* measure which simply brought together in a tidy form the 1893 Act as it had been amended between 1893 and 1979 and made no changes in the law. With only a couple of exceptions indeed the section numbers of the 1893 and 1979 Acts are identical.

The law of sale of goods is for the most part, therefore, an exposition of the effect of the Sale of Goods Act 1979 but it is probably not the case that all the answers are to be found in the Act.

A further difficulty is that although sale is by far the most important contract under which goods are supplied it is not the only one. There are in fact many ways in which goods may be supplied and in some cases the boundaries between them may have legal consequences. These problems are discussed in Chapter 2.

2 THE BORDERLINE BETWEEN CONTRACT LAW AND SALES LAW

1-03

Not all the legal problems which arise in relation to a contract for the sale of goods are part of the law of sale of goods. Many must be solved by applying the general law of contract. So, for instance, the question of whether there is a contract at all is primarily a matter for the general law of contract. Although all lawyers would agree that this distinction between the general law of contract and the special law of sale of goods exists, there would be many different answers as to where precisely the boundary lies. This book is not a discussion of the general law of contract but of the special rules affecting the sale of goods and other contracts for the supply of goods. In practice, however, legal rules do not exist in watertight compartments and from time to time it will not be possible to explain the legal position without discussing the general law

---

[1]   [1891] A.C. 107.

of contract. Indeed the draftsman of the Sale of Goods Act had the same problem. A number of the provisions of the Act, for instance those about damages, appear to be simply applications of general contract principles to the specific case of sale of goods. Most of the time the distinction between general contract law and special sales law has no more importance that this. Occasionally, however, the relationship between general and special rules assumes practical significance. An example is *Cehave v. Bremer, The Hansa Nord* (1976)[2]. This case concerned the buyer's right to reject defective goods.

1-04

The contract was for the sale of citrus pulp pellets, which were to be used for feeding animals. It was an express term of the contract that the goods should be shipped in good condition. It was accepted that the goods shipped were not in good condition though the defects were relatively minor and the pellets were in fact eventually used for cattle feed. The buyer claimed to be entitled to reject the goods. His principal argument was that all terms in a contract of sale of goods are either conditions or warranties and that the buyer is entitled to reject the goods if the term broken by the seller is a condition; the term that the goods be shipped in good condition was one, a breach of which would often be serious, and therefore it should be classified as a condition. This argument appeared to derive a good deal of support from the Sale of Goods Act 1893 since in that Act, all the terms which are classified are classified as either conditions or warranties. Indeed, between 1893 and 1962 it was widely thought to be a general principle of contract law that all terms of a contract were either conditions or warranties. However, the Court of Appeal rejected the argument. Instead it argued that under general contract law there were three categories of terms, conditions, warranties and innominate terms; that the *Cehave v. Bremer* case was governed by general contract law and that the relevant rules must be the same for sale as for other contracts.

This complex and difficult technical question will be discussed in more detail later (Chapter 8). The important point to emphasise for present purposes is that the Court of Appeal was able to reach the result it desired by classifying the matter in dispute as one of general contract law.

3 IS THE SALE OF GOODS ACT A COMPLETE CODE?

It seems likely that Sir MacKenzie Chalmers intended the Sale of Goods Act 1893 to contain all the special rules about the sale of goods.

1-05

---

2   [1976] Q.B. 44.

He was certainly well aware of the problems discussed in the last section and dealt with them by providing in s. 62(2) that:

> '... the rules of the common law, including the law merchant, save in so far as they are inconsistent with the provisions of this Act, and in particular the rules relating to the law of principal and agent and the effect of fraud, misrepresentation, duress or coercion, mistake or other invalidating cause, apply to contracts for the sale of goods.'

In *Re Wait* (1927)[3] Atkin LJ clearly took the view that where a matter was dealt with by the Act, the treatment was intended to be exhaustive. He said 'The total sum of legal relations ... arising out of the contract for the sale of goods may well be regarded as defined by the code.' The question in that case was whether the buyer could obtain specific performance of the contract. Section 52 of the Sale of Goods Act says that a buyer may obtain specific performance of a contract for the sale of specific or ascertained goods. (These terms are explained in 'Specific and Unascertained Goods', Chapter 3.) The Act does not expressly say that specific performance cannot be obtained where the goods are not specific or ascertained but Atkin LJ thought that s. 52 should be treated as a complete statement of the circumstances in which specific performance should be granted for a contract of sale of goods. On the other hand in the more recent case of *Sky Petroleum Ltd. v. VIP Petroleum Ltd.* (1974)[4] Goulding J thought that he had jurisdiction to grant specific performance in such a case, though the views of Atkin LJ do not appear to have been drawn to his attention.

The problem was discussed again, though not decided, in *Leigh and Sillivan Ltd. v. Aliakmon Shipping Co. Ltd.* (1986)[5] where Lord Brandon of Oakbrook stated that his provisional view accorded with that expressed by Atkin LJ in *Re Wait*.

4 DOMESTIC AND INTERNATIONAL SALES

1-06   Most of the cases discussed in this book will concern domestic sales, that is, sales where the buyer the seller and the goods are all present in England and Wales. Obviously there are many international sales which have no connection at all with English law. However, there are many international sales which are governed by English law, either because English law is the law most closely connected with the transaction or because the parties have chosen English law as the governing law. It is in

---

3   [1927] 1 Ch. 606.
4   [1974] 1 All E.R. 954; [1974] 1 W.L.R. 576.
5   [1986] 1 All E.R. 146; [1986] 1 A.C. 785.

fact common for parties expressly to choose English law because of a desire to have the transaction governed by English law or for disputes to be litigated or arbitrated in England. So many transactions in the grain or sugar trades will be subject to English law by reason of the parties' choice although neither the seller nor the buyer nor the goods ever comes near England.

In general where an international sale transaction is subject to English law, it will be subject to the provisions of the Sale of Goods Act. However, in practice a solution which makes good commercial sense for domestic sales may make much less good sense for international sales and of course vice versa. So although the Act says that risk *prima facie* passes with property, a rule which is often applied in domestic sales, in practice it is extremely common in international sales for risk and property to pass at different moments. Furthermore, most international sales involve use of documents, particularly of the Bill of Lading, and often involve payment by letter of credit which is virtually unknown in domestic sales. The rules set out in this text should therefore only be applied with great caution in the context of international sales, which really needs to be studied as a separate subject.

5 COMMERCIAL AND CONSUMER SALES

The Sale of Goods Act 1893 was predominantly based on Chalmers' careful reading of the 19th-century cases on sales. These cases are almost entirely concerned with commercial transactions, particularly relatively small scale commodity sales. Few consumer transactions, except perhaps sales of horses, figure in this body of case law. It is true that the 1893 Act has some provisions which only apply where the seller is selling in the course of a business but these provisions do not discriminate according to whether the buyer is buying as a business or as a consumer. For the most part this is still true though the modern consumer movement has meant that we now have a number of statutory provisions which are designed to protect consumers either in circumstances where it is assumed that businessmen can protect themselves or that they need less by way of protection. These developments are particularly important in relation to defective goods and to exemption clauses.

CHAPTER 2

TYPES OF TRANSACTION

This chapter considers the different ways in which the act of supplying goods may take place. It is largely descriptive but some legal consequences flow from the choice of transaction and these are pointed out.

1 NON-CONTRACTUAL SUPPLY

Usually where goods are supplied there will be a contract between the supplier and the receiver of the goods. Most of this chapter is taken up with considering the various kinds of contract which can be involved but it should be noted first that a contract is not essential.

The most obvious case where there is no contract is where there is a gift. In English law, promises to make gifts in the future are not binding unless they are made under seal (for example covenants in favour of charities) but a gift, once executed, will be effective to transfer ownership from donor to donee provided that the appropriate form has been used. So, in principle, effective gifts of goods require physical handing over though no doubt in the case of a bulky object like a car, it would be sufficient to hand over the keys as the effective means of control. A major difference between gifts and other forms of supply is that the legal responsibility of the donor for the condition of the goods is relatively slight. It will be pointed out in Chapter 8 that most suppliers of goods make implied undertakings about the quality of the goods but in the case of a gift the donor's liability is probably limited to warning of known dangerous defects in the goods. So if I give away my car, I ought to warn the donee if I know that the brakes do not work but I shall not be liable if the engine seizes up after two hundred miles.

In some cases a donee may have an action against the manufacturers. So, if I give my wife a hair dryer for her birthday and it burns her hair because it has been badly wired, she will not have an action against me except in the unlikely case that I knew of the defect. In most cases the retail shop which supplies the goods would be in breach of their contract with me but I would not have suffered the loss, whereas my wife, who has suffered the loss, has no contract with them. However, she could sue the manufacturer if she could prove that the hair dryer had been negligently manufactured. It is a curious feature of

7

the present law that my wife would legally be much better off if I had given her the money to buy the hair dryer for herself.

2-02   It can be surprisingly difficult to decide whether or not a transaction is a gift. Many promotional schemes make use of so-called gifts; can customers complain if they do not receive the gift? Often the answer seems to be yes. The question was examined by the House of Lords in *Esso Petroleum v. Customs and Excise* (1976)[1].

In this case Esso devised a marketing scheme which was linked to the England squad for the 1970 World Cup in Mexico. Coins were provided, each of which bore the head and shoulders of a member of the squad. Prominent signs were placed in Esso filling stations stating that those who bought four gallons of petrol would receive a coin and books were given away in which sets of coins could be collected. The legal analysis of this scheme arose in an unexpected way. The Customs and Excise claimed that the coins were subject to purchase tax. This tax (effectively the predecessor of VAT) was due if the coins were produced for the purpose of being sold. The scheme had been so successful that although each coin was of minimal value, over £100,000 would have been due if the Customs and Excise had won the case. Esso argued that the coins were being given away so that the customer who bought four gallons would have no legal right to the coins. In the House of Lords this argument failed although only by three votes to two. The majority view was that the customer would have a legitimate expectation of receiving a coin, even though in practice it was very unlikely that a disappointed customer would go to court and pursue a claim. However, Esso succeeded with a second line of argument. Of the three judges who held that the coins were supplied under contract, two were persuaded that the transaction involved was not one contract. According to this analysis the customer bought the petrol under a conventional contract of sale and there was a separate contract under which the filling station owner undertook to transfer a coin for every four gallons bought. The legal point of this was that this second contract was not a contract of sale since the coin was not being bought for money and purchase tax was only due if the coins were being produced for the purpose of being sold.

Even where it is clear that money will change hands, the transaction is not necessarily contractual. An important example is the supply of prescribed drugs under the National Health Service. Although for many patients there is now a substantial charge, the House of Lords held in *Pfizer Corp. v. Minister of Health* (1965)[2] that there is no contract. The basic reason for this is that a contract depends on agreement, even though the

---

[1]   [1976] 1 All E.R. 117; [1976] 1 W.L.R. 1.
[2]   [1965] A.C. 512.

element of agreement is often somewhat attenuated in prac
patient's right to the drugs and the pharmacist's duty to disper
depend on agreement but on statute. Similar reasoning applies
utilities, such as the supply of water (*Read v. Croydon Corporation* (1938)[3]).

2 SALE OF GOODS

Section 2 of the Sale of Goods Act 1979 defines a contract of sale of **2-03**
goods as 'a contract by which the seller transfers or agrees to transfer the
property in goods to the buyer for a money consideration called the
price'. It follows that this is essentially a transaction in which one side
promises to transfer the ownership of goods and the other pays the price
in money. This therefore excludes cases where there is no money price
and situations where what is sold is not goods but land or what is often
called intangible property, that is property interests which cannot be
physically possessed such as shares, patents, copyrights and so on (this
is discussed further in Chapter 3).

It is one of the features of English law that quite different regimes
apply to contracts for the sale of land and the sale of goods. So, for
instance, while sellers of goods are under extensive implied liability as to
the quality of these goods, sellers of land are liable only for their express
undertakings as to quality. Usually of course there is no difficulty in
deciding whether the contract is one for the sale of land or for the sale of
goods but there are some borderline problems in relation to growing
crops or minerals under the land. Under s. 61(1) of the Sale of Goods Act
1979 a contract for crops or minerals is a contract for the sale of goods if
they are to be severed from the land either 'before the sale or under the
contract of sale'. On the other hand a contract for the sale of a farm
would normally be treated as a contract for the sale of land even though
there were growing crops.

In some cases however the court might treat the transaction as two
contracts, one for the sale of the farm and the other for the sale of the
crops. So in *English Hop Growers v. Dering* (1928)[4] the defendant (the
owner of a hop farm) had agreed to sell hops only to the plaintiff. The
defendant sold the farm when the hop crop was nearing maturity and
the court analysed the transaction as being two contracts, one for the sale
of the farm and the other for the sale of the hops. The practical result was
that the defendant was in breach of the contract with the plaintiff. If the
transaction had been treated as a single contract the result would have
been different for the defendant had not promised not to sell the farm.

---

3   [1938] 4 All E.R. 632.
4   [1928] 2 K.B. 174.

3 EXCHANGE

2-04   The requirement in s. 2 of the 1979 Act that there must be a money price in a sale means that an exchange of a cow for a horse is not a sale. For most purposes this makes no great practical difference because the courts are likely to apply rules similar to the Sale of Goods Act by analogy. Between 1677 and 1954 contracts for the sale of goods worth £10 or more required to be evidenced in writing. This requirement was never applied to exchanges so that many of the older cases arose in this context. Straightforward exchange or barter does not appear to be very common in domestic trade though it is increasingly common in international trade because one of the parties is short of hard currency. On the other hand part exchange is very common, particularly in relation to motor cars. This raises the question of the correct classification of an agreement to exchange a new car for an old one plus £2,000. In practice this is often solved by the way that the parties write up the contract. In many cases they will price each car so that the natural analysis is that there are two sales with an agreement to pay the balance in cash. This was how the transaction was approached in *Aldridge v. Johnson* (1857)[5] where 32 bullocks valued at £192 were to be transferred by one party and 100 quarters of barley valued at £215 to be transferred by the other.

Many new for old car trades would be susceptible to this two contract approach. An alternative approach would be that the new car was being sold but that the customer was given the option of tendering the old car in part payment rather than paying the whole price in cash. Customary practices as to part exchange prices would usually make this a more attractive option to the buyer. Sales where the buyer has the option to do or deliver something in partial substitution for the price are by no means unusual. Such an option does not convert the transaction from a sale to an exchange.

Where the component elements of the deal are not separately priced, it is obviously difficult to adopt this analysis. So if in *Aldridge v. Johnson* the agreement had simply been one for 32 bullocks and £23 to be transferred on one hand and 100 quarters of barley on the other the transaction would have been properly classified as an exchange. It is possible that if the money element in the exchange was predominant and the goods element a makeweight the transaction should be regarded as a sale but this situation seems never to have been litigated in England.

---

5   (1857) 7 E&B 855.

Exchange is usually discussed in relation to transfer of goods by each party but the same principles would seem to apply where goods are transferred in exchange for services.

4 CONTRACTS FOR WORK AND MATERIALS

Many contracts which are undoubtedly contracts of sale include an element of service. So if I go to a tailor and buy a suit off the peg, the tailor may agree to raise one of the shoulders since one of my shoulders is higher than the other. The contract would still be one of sale. Conversely, if I take my car to the garage for a service, the garage may fit some new parts but such a transaction would not normally be regarded as a sale. Of course, in both these cases the parties could, if they wished, divide the transaction up into two contracts, one of which would be a contract of sale and the other a contract of services, but in practice this is not usually done.

2-05

It is clear that there are many contracts in which goods are supplied as part of a package which also includes the provision of services. Some are treated as contracts of sale; others are treated as a separate category called contracts for work and materials. Again, this distinction was important between 1677 and 1954 because contracts of sale over £10 required to be evidenced in writing whereas contracts for work and materials did not. Since 1954 the distinction is less important because although the Sale of Goods Act does not apply to contracts for work and materials, similar rules are usually applied by analogy. This is perhaps as well, since it is far from clear where the line between sale and work and materials is to be drawn.

In some cases it is possible to say that the property transfer element is so predominant that the contract is clearly one of sale; in others the work element is so large that it is obviously work and materials. This approach seems to work with the off the peg suit (sale) and car service (work and materials) examples above but what is the position where there is a substantial element both of property transfer and work?

Unfortunately, in the two leading cases the courts adopted different tests. In *Lee v. Griffin* (1861)[6] a contract by a dentist to make and fit dentures for a patient was said to be a contract of sale on the ground that at the end of the day there was a discernible article which was to be transferred from the dentist to the patient. On the other hand, in

---

6   (1861) 1 B&S 272.

Robinson v. Graves (1935)[7] it was said that a contract to paint a portrait was one for work and materials because 'the substance of the contract is the skill and experience of the artist in producing a picture'. These tests appear irreconcilable.

2-06   The way in which the parties have set up the transaction may sometimes solve the problem of classification. If I select a length of cloth from my tailor, pay for it and then ask for a suit to be made up from it, a court is very likely to say that there are two contracts, one to buy the cloth and the other to make the suit. In commercial life it is quite common for the customer to provide the materials from which goods are produced. The free issue of materials is discussed below.

Where the contract is classified as one for work and materials, the supplier's obligations as to the quality of the goods will be virtually identical to those of the seller since the terms to be implied under the Supply of Goods and Services Act 1982 are the same as those to be implied under the Sale of Goods Act 1979. It is worth explaining, however, that the supplier's obligation as to the quality of the work will often be substantially different from that concerning the quality of the materials. This can be simply illustrated with the everyday case of taking a car to a garage for a service. Let us suppose that during the service the garage supplies and fits a new tyre to the car. As far as fitting is concerned, the garage's obligation is to ensure that the tyre is fitted with reasonable care and skill. However, it may be that the tyre though fitted carefully contains a defect of manufacture not apparent to visual inspection which leads to a blow-out when the car is being driven at speed on the motorway. The garage will be liable for this defect because the tyre was not merchantable or reasonably fit for its purpose and this liability is quite independent of any fault on the part of the garage owner.

5 CONSTRUCTION CONTRACTS

2-07   In most respects a contract with a builder to build a house is very like a contract with a tailor to make a suit. In both cases property in the raw materials will pass but the skills deployed in converting the raw materials into the finished product appear to make up the greater part of the transaction. There is one obvious difference however. A contract to buy a ready made suit is clearly a contract for the sale of goods but a contract for a house already built is a contract for the sale of land. This has meant that the seller of a house does not normally undertake the implied obligations as to the quality of the product which are undertaken

---

7   [1935] 1 K.B. 579.

by the seller of goods. It is perhaps doubtful whether this distinction is sensible since it seems to be based on historical factors rather than on any underlying policy reasons. In modern practice the purchaser of a new house will often be offered an express guarantee as for instance under the NHBC scheme and the prudent purchaser of a second-hand house will have it surveyed although this will not protect against defects which the reasonably competent surveyor could not be expected to discover.

However, although English law treats sales of 'off the peg' suits and houses quite differently, it treats the contract to make suits and build houses very similarly since it will imply into a contract to build a house terms as to the quality of the materials and workmanship. So, in *Young and Marten Ltd. v. McManus Childs Ltd.* (1969)[8], a contract for the erection of a building required the builders to use 'Somerset 13' tiles on the roof. They obtained a supply of these tiles (which were only made by one manufacturer) and fixed them with reasonable skill. Unfortunately, the batch of tiles proved to be faulty and let in the rain. The House of Lords held that the builders were in breach of their implied obligations as to fitness for purpose.

6 FREE ISSUE OF MATERIALS

Tailors who make suits to measure tend to have lengths of suitable cloth in stock. However, not everyone who is in the business of making up something will find it convenient to hold stocks of materials. It may be commercially more satisfactory for the customer to provide the material. This leads to the phenomenon often called free issue of materials, for example, a customer may collect supplies of steel from a stockholder and deliver them to a fabricator for making up according to a specification. On the face of it this transaction does not involve any changes in ownership since the steel already belongs to the customer when it is handed to the fabricator. Such a contract would therefore be one for the fabricator's services.

    2-08

The position might be different where the raw materials were invoiced to the supplier and the finished product then invoiced back to the customer. This will often support an inference that the customer had sold the raw materials and was buying the finished product.

The most difficult case is perhaps when the finished product is made up partly from materials supplied by the maker and partly from those supplied by the customer. The solution appears to lie in deciding which are the principal materials.

---

8   [1969] 1 A.C. 454.

7 HIRE-PURCHASE

2-09   It seems likely that buyers have always been keener to get the goods than to pay for them, but undoubtedly one of the features of the modern consumer society is the extent of the credit explosion fuelled by a deliberate decision by suppliers to encourage consumers to acquire goods on credit rather than for cash. This leads to all sorts of problems which are outside the scope of this book but it is necessary to notice the effect on the range of possible transactions.

One of the risks that a seller who supplies on credit runs is that the customer will fail to pay. A natural response to this is to provide that if the buyer does not keep up the payments the seller can repossess the goods. It is not necessarily sufficient, however, to rely on a contractual right to repossess since a customer who is a bad payer may have other financial problems and could become insolvent leading to any asset being divided up amongst all the creditors. In order to guard against this possibility a seller may provide that the goods are to remain his or her property until the buyer has paid for them in full and to a large extent this will protect against the buyer's insolvency (this is discussed more fully in Chapter 6).

A buyer who is hard up may not simply fail to keep up the payments but may sell the goods in order to raise some cash. Although a buyer who has not yet become the owner should not do this, such a sale will often be effective to transfer ownership to the sub-buyer (Chapter 6). In the 1890s ingenious lawyers were seeking a way to prevent the seller's rights being defeated in this way and invented the contract of hire-purchase.

Under this contract the customer agrees to hire the goods for a period (usually two or three years) and has an option to buy them at the end of this period, usually for a nominal additional sum. The economic expectation of the parties is that the customer will exercise this option and indeed the rate charged for hire will be calculated on the basis of the cash price of the goods plus a handsome rate of interest and not on the market rate for hiring them. Nevertheless, the customer does not actually contract to buy the goods and the House of Lords held in *Helby v. Matthews* (1895)[9] that the contract was not one of sale and that a sale by the hirer before all the instalments had been paid did not operate to transfer ownership to the sub-buyer. The effect of this decision was that although economically and commercially a contract of hire-purchase had the same objectives as a credit sale, its legal effect was fundamentally different.

---

[9]   [1895] A.C. 471.

A further oddity of hire-purchase is that, particularly in the case of motor cars, the finance does not actually come from the supplier but from a finance company, that is a body whose commercial purpose is to lend money and not to supply goods. The position may be represented diagrammatically as follows:

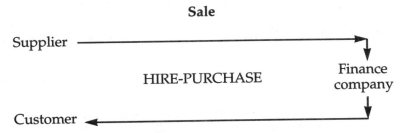

Sale

Supplier

HIRE-PURCHASE   Finance
company

Customer

The customer may often think that the goods are being bought on credit from the supplier whereas, in fact, they are being acquired on hire-purchase from the finance company. Typically, the supplier will have the finance company's standard forms which will be completed for the customer to sign. These will usually amount to an offer to sell the car to the finance company and an offer by the customer to take the car on hire-purchase terms. Both contracts will come into existence when the finance company decides to adopt the transaction. In the standard situation there is indeed no contract between the supplier and the customer, though courts have been willing to discover such a contract with relative ease. For instance, in *Andrews v. Hopkinson* (1957)[10] a car dealer said to a customer 'It is a good little bus; I would stake my life on it.' This was held to be a contractually binding warranty. In that case the contract between dealer and customer was what lawyers call a 'collateral' contract, that is, one dependent on the main contract between the finance company and customer. Implicitly the dealer is treated as saying 'If you take this car on hire-purchase terms from the finance company, I will guarantee it.'

Instead of taking the car on hire-purchase terms the customer might go to a bank for a personal loan in order to buy the car for cash. In substance this would be a very similar transaction; the interest charged would be comparable and indeed many of the finance companies are owned by banks. It will be seen, however, that the legal form is very different. This artificiality has been the source of many difficulties, some of which will be considered later.

---

10   [1957] 1 Q.B. 229.

From the 1890s onwards hire-purchase became a very popular technique for supplying goods on credit. It has been widely used in consumer transactions but is by no means unknown in commercial ones. It has always co-existed with conditional sales, that is, transactions where the supplier delivers goods but on condition that the ownership shall remain in the seller until all instalments have been paid. The modern tendency embodied in the comprehensive and complex Consumer Credit Act 1974 is to treat all forms of instalment credit in the same way.

8 HIRE

2-11   In practice whether the contract is one for sale, exchange, work and materials or hire-purchase the customer will end up as the owner of the goods. However, the customer may be more concerned with the use than the ownership of the goods. One reason for this could be that only short term use is intended, for example, a car which is hired for a week's holiday. But there may be other reasons. Many British families choose to rent rather than buy a television despite countless articles demonstrating that if the television lasts for more than three years it is cheaper to buy it than to rent it. Perhaps the most plausible reason for this is the belief that rental companies offer better service than sellers or independent repairers.

A contract in which goods are transferred from the owner to a user for a time with the intention that they will be returned later is a contract of hire. It is an essential part of such a contract that the possession of the goods is transferred. So a number of transactions which would colloquially be described as hire are not accurately so-called. For instance, one might well talk of hiring a bus for a school outing but this would not strictly be correct if, as would usually be the case, the bus came with a driver. In that case the owner would remain in possession through the driver and the contract would be simply one for use of the bus. The position is the same in a commercial context where a piece of plant such as a bulldozer or a crane is supplied with an operator except where, as is often the case, the operator is transferred with the equipment and becomes for the time being the employee of the hirer. In this latter case it would be accurate to describe the transaction as hire.

9 LEASES

2-12   In recent years it has been common for contracts for the use of goods to be made and described as 'leases'. So a car may be 'leased' rather than bought as may major items of office equipment or computers. There can be a number of advantages in this from the customer's point of view. One is that such transactions appear to be of an income rather than a capital nature so they will not show up in the company's balance sheet as a capital purchase. This can be attractive as it may make the company's financial position look better. Nor is this necessarily a cosmetic benefit since there can be perfectly good business reasons for wishing to avoid tying up capital in equipment, particularly where it has to be borrowed at high rates of interest. Apart from these financial advantages, there may also be tax benefits for a business in leasing equipment rather than buying it.

Although the term 'lease' is very commonly used to describe such transactions, there is at present no separate legal category of leases of goods, unlike leases of land which have been recognised from the 12th century. Therefore, in law, most leases will simply be contracts of hire. In some cases, however, there may be an understanding that at the end of the period of the lease the customer may or will buy the goods. This may amount to no more than a non-binding arrangement in which case it will have no effect on the legal nature of the transaction. If, however, the customer has an option to buy the goods at the end of the lease, the transaction will in substance be one of hire-purchase. If the customer has agreed to buy the goods at the end of the lease then it would seem that the contract is actually one of sale.

It is worth noting that in many 'leases' the 'lessor' is not the supplier but a bank or finance house. In such cases the supplier sells the goods to a bank which then leases them to the customer. This produces a triangular relationship like that in a hire-purchase contract, shown diagrammatically at para 2-09. This rather artificial arrangement can give rise to difficulties, particularly when the goods turn out to be defective. It is natural to assume that the supplier is the person primarily responsible for the quality of the goods but the fact that there is usually no contract between the supplier and the customer makes it difficult to give effect to this assumption. The lessor would be under implied obligations as to the quality of the goods but it is likely to have attempted in its standard form of lease to escape from these obligations.

10   PRACTICAL SIGNIFICANCE OF THESE DISTINCTIONS

2-13

Many readers may feel that this quite elaborate catalogue of different transactions is a typical example of the passion of lawyers to make things more complicated. The practical difficulty is the predominance of statute law in this area. Each of the statutes deals with a particular contract and it is therefore necessary to it. This is particularly so with the

Sale of Goods Act 1979 which applies only to contracts for the sale of goods strictly defined and which is much the most important statute in the field.

Judges have reduced these difficulties in practice by being willing in some cases to apply the rules of the Sale of Goods Act by analogy to other contracts. This was particularly true in relation to implied undertakings as to the ownership and quality of the goods and Parliament adopted this approach in 1982 when it passed the Supply of Goods and Services Act which provided for implied terms as to ownership and quality in contracts of exchange and work and materials, which were in identical terms to those contained in the Sale of Goods Act.

Nevertheless, the 1982 Act only dealt with these problems and important as they are they make up only a proportion of the whole. No doubt in some other areas judges will solve problems by applying the Sale of Goods Act 1979 by analogy. This technique works best where the solution can, at least in theory, be explained as turning on the implied understanding of the parties but there are some provisions in the Sale of Goods Act which cannot possibly be explained in such a way (see particularly the rules discussed in Chapter 6).

4 oO1323

MEANING AND TYPES OF GOODS

This chapter deals with some basic definitions. This is not very exciting but it is essential to understand what follows.

1 THE DEFINITION OF GOODS

Section 61(1) of the Sale of Goods Act 1979 states that goods: **3-01**

'Includes all personal chattels other than things in action and money, [and in Scotland all corporeal moveables except money] and in particular "goods" includes emblements, industrial growing crops, and things attached to or forming part of the land which are agreed to be severed before sale or under the contract of sale.'

The words in brackets reflect the different legal terminology of Scotland and may be ignored for present purposes. The remainder of the text uses some unfamiliar English and requires further explanation.

Historically, English lawyers have divided property into 'real property' (basically land) and 'personal property' (all forms of wealth other than land). This terminology has found its way into ordinary usage. In origin real property was property which could be recovered by a real action, that is an action which leads to the recovery of property *in specie* and not to damages for its non return. Unfortunately, when this distinction was first drawn (in the 12th century) only freehold estates could be recovered by real action. Purists therefore took the view that leasehold estates were not real property. By the 15th century leasehold interests were as effectively protected by the courts as freehold interests but the terminology survived and leasehold interests were called 'chattels real'. This terminology is now archaic but it survived long enough to influence the definition in 1893 and the 1979 Act simply repeats the wording of the 1893 Act.

Etymologically, the words 'chattel' and 'cattle' appear to be different spellings of the same old Norman French word, which meant property but over the centuries 'cattle' has been narrowed to its modern meaning of livestock while the word 'chattel' has retained its wider meaning. So 'personal chattels' would mean all forms of property other than 'real property' (freehold interests in land) and 'chattels real' (leasehold interests in land). The Act goes on specifically to exclude 'things in action' and 'money'. 'Things in action' are those forms of property which cannot be physically possessed so that they can only be enjoyed by bringing an action. This includes such things as shares, patents, copyrights, trademarks, rights under bills of exchange and policies of insurance. The exclusion of 'money' presumably means that a contract to purchase foreign exchange is not a sale of goods. On the other hand a contract to purchase banknotes issued by the Confederate States of America probably is a contract for the sale of goods since the notes will have been bought for their historic interest and are no longer usable as currency.

The second half of the definition deals with the case of the sale of growing crops, etc., which has already been discussed.

2   EXISTING AND FUTURE GOODS

3-02   The Sale of Goods Act 1979 contains two explicit sets of subdivisions of goods. One is existing and future goods and the other specific and unascertained goods (discussed in Specific and Unascertained goods, below). Section 5(1) says that:

'The goods which form the subject of a contract of sale may be either existing goods, owned or possessed by the seller, or goods to be manufactured or acquired by him after the making of the contract of sale, in this Act called future goods.'

Future goods are also defined by s. 61(1) as:

'... goods to be manufactured or acquired by the seller after the making of the contract of sale.'

It will be seen that goods which are in existence may be future goods as where the seller has agreed to sell goods which at the time of the contract are owned by someone else. A typical example of future goods would arise where the seller was to make the goods but the category would appear also to include things which will come into existence naturally as where a dog breeder agrees to sell a puppy from the litter of a pregnant bitch. In such a case there is an element of risk that things will not turn out as the parties hope; for instance that all the puppies die or that the buyer had contracted for a dog puppy and all the puppies are bitches. In such a case the court will have to analyse the agreement to see whether the seller's agreement was conditional on there being a live puppy or a puppy of the right sex.

3 SPECIFIC AND UNASCERTAINED GOODS

Section 61(1) defines 'specific goods' as 'goods identified and agreed on at the time a contract of sale is made'.   **3-03**

Unascertained goods are not defined by the Act but it is clear that goods which are not specific are unascertained. It is important to emphasise that the distinction relates to the position at the time the contract of sale is made. Later events will not make the goods specific but they may, and often will, make them ascertained.

As we shall see (Chapter 6) the distinction between specific and unascertained goods is of particular importance in the passing of property between seller and buyer. It may prove helpful therefore to explain further that unascertained goods may be of at least three different kinds. One possibility is that the goods are to be manufactured by the seller. Here they will usually become ascertained as a result of the process of manufacture though if the seller is making similar goods for two or more buyers some further acts may be necessary to make it clear which goods have been appropriated to which buyer. The second possibility is that the goods are sold by a generic description such as '500 tons Western White Wheat'. In such a case the seller could perform the contract by delivering any 500 tons of Western White Wheat (provided that it was of merchantable quality, etc.). If the seller was a trader in wheat, he or she might well have more than 500 tons of wheat but would not be bound to use that wheat to perform the contract; he or she could and often would choose to buy further wheat on the market to fulfil the order. Where there is an active market sellers and buyers may be entering into a complex series of sales and purchases according to their perception of how the market is moving and leaving who gets what wheat to be sorted out later. This is obviously particularly likely where the sales are for delivery at some future date rather than for immediate despatch. In this situation the seller may form plans to use a parcel of wheat to deliver to buyer A and another parcel to buyer B. Usually, the forming of these plans will not make the goods ascertained until the seller makes some act of appropriation which prevents a change of mind.

A third and perhaps less obvious possibility is that the goods may   **3-04**
be part of an undivided bulk. So if the seller has 1,000 tons of Western White Wheat on board the SS Challenger and sells 500 tons to A and 500 tons to B these are sales of unascertained goods since it is not possible to tell which 500 tons has been sold to which purchaser. Important practical consequences flow from this rule: in this situation the goods become ascertained only when it can be established which part of the cargo is appropriated to which contract. So in *Karlhamns*

Oljefabriker v. Eastport Navigation (1982)[1] 22,000 tons of copra were loaded on board a ship in the Philippines, of which 6,000 tons were sold to a Swedish buyer. At this stage, of course, the goods were unascertained. The ship called at Rotterdam and at Hamburg on its way to Sweden and 16,000 tons were offloaded at these two ports. It was held that the goods became ascertained on the completion of discharge in Hamburg as it was then possible to say with certainty that the remainder of the cargo was destined for the purchaser.

This rule will be significantly modified if the Sale of Goods Bill 1995 becomes law. Under the terms of this Bill as it stands at the time of writing, if a seller sells part of an undivided bulk, the buyer may become a tenant in common of a proportional share of the whole bulk.

4 SALES AND AGREEMENTS TO SELL

3-05

Section 2 of the Sale of Goods Act 1979 draws a distinction between sales and agreements to sell. Section 2(4) provides:

'Where under a contract of sale the property in the goods is transferred from the seller to the buyer the contract is called a sale.'

Section 2(5) states:

'Where under a contract of sale the transfer of the property in the goods is to take place at a future time or subject to some condition later to be fulfilled, the contract is called an agreement to sell.'

The reason for this distinction arises from an ambiguity in the word 'sale' which may refer either to the contract between buyer and seller or to the transfer of ownership from seller to buyer which is the object of the agreement. In English law it is possible, in principle, for ownership to pass from seller to buyer simply by agreement without either delivery of the goods or payment of the price.

---

1   [1982] 1 All E.R. 208.

CHAPTER 4

THE PRICE

1 INTRODUCTION

In a contract of sale the irreducible minimum of obligations is for the **4-01** seller to deliver the goods and the buyer to pay the price. This chapter considers the rules about the ascertainment of the price and Chapter 5 describes the rules about payment of the price and delivery of the goods.

Sections 8 and 9 of the Sale of Goods Act 1979 deal with the price. Section 8 provides:

'(1)   The price in a contract of sale may be fixed by the contract, or may be left to be fixed in a manner agreed by the contract, or may be determined by the course of dealings between the parties.

(2)   Where the price is not determined as mentioned in sub-section (1) above the buyer must pay a reasonable price.

(3)   What is a reasonable price is a question of fact dependent on the circumstances of each particular case.'

Section 9 states:

'(1)   Where there is an agreement to sell goods on the terms that the price is to be fixed by the valuation of a third party, and he cannot or does not make the valuation, the agreement is avoided; but if the goods or any part of them have been delivered to and appropriated by the buyer he must pay a reasonable price for them.

(2)   Where the third party is prevented from making the valuation by the fault of the seller or buyer, the party not at fault may maintain an action for damages against the party at fault.'

These sections do not appear in fact to cover all the difficulties that can arise and in practice resort is also made to the general principles of contract law.

2 THE PARTIES SAY NOTHING ABOUT THE PRICE

The fact that no price has been agreed might be good evidence that **4-02** the parties had not completed a contract but it is clear that in practice people often make binding contracts without having agreed on the payment terms. Many people will ask a solicitor to handle the buying or selling of their house without agreeing or even asking about the cost, though the practice of asking for an estimate and 'shopping around' is becoming more widespread. Similarly, a customer may ring up an established supplier and ask for certain specified goods to be sent round without asking the price. In such a case it is clear that there is a contract to buy at a reasonable price (s. 8(2)).

Section 8(3) of the Sale of Goods Act 1979 says that what is a reasonable price is a question of fact. If the seller is in business evidence of his or her usual prices will be good evidence of what is a reasonable price but in theory at least it is not decisive. Undoubtedly however the scope for arguing that the seller's usual prices are not reasonable must be limited in some cases. If a Chelsea housewife telephones an order to Harrods Food Hall it may be doubted whether she can resist paying their standard charges on the ground that she could have bought the goods more cheaply at a supermarket. No doubt one reason for this is that a court would be entitled to take into account the size, location and expense of the seller's premises and the quality of service offered in deciding what was reasonable. Another different argument pointing to the same result would be that it is the universal practice of English grocers to price the goods on their shelves so that customers may reasonably expect that all goods will be sold at marked prices, no more and no less.

Obviously, however, there are sales where the seller is not in business or not in the business of selling goods of the kind sold. In such cases there will be no seller's standard price to appeal to and the court will have to do the best it can with such evidence as the parties present to it.

3 THE PARTIES FIX THE PRICE IN THE CONTRACT

4-03 This is the simplest and probably most common situation. Obviously the parties may fix the price in a number of different ways. I may sell my car for £3,000 but if I take the car to the filling station I would ask for as much petrol as was needed to fill the tank at 55p a litre; in the first case a global price and in the second a unit price. It may make sense in some cases to fix a price in relation to some objective external measure. For example, 1,000 barrels of oil delivered on 1 December 1993 at the best price quoted that day on the Rotterdam spot market.

An important point often overlooked in practice is what the price includes. Retail sellers are usually obliged to quote VAT inclusive prices but in most other cases prices are VAT exclusive unless otherwise agreed. It may be important to know whether the price covers packing and delivery. Such matters are covered in well drafted conditions of sale and purchase but are otherwise often forgotten.

4 THE PRICE IS LEFT TO BE FIXED IN A MANNER AGREED BY THE CONTRACT

Section 8(1) of the Sale of Goods Act 1979 clearly contemplates that the contract may leave the prices to be fixed later in an agreed manner. One such manner would be third party valuation but this is expressly dealt with by s. 9 and is discussed separately below. The act is silent on other methods of price fixing and the matter is not free from difficulties.

4-04

One possibility is that the contract may provide for the price to be fixed by the seller (or the buyer). At first sight it seems strange for one party to agree that the price is to be fixed by the other but such contracts are in fact quite common. A classic example is the contracts made by oil companies to supply petrol to filling stations. These are nearly all on a long term basis because the companies are anxious to have guaranteed outlets. Typically therefore, filling station operators agree to take all their supplies of petrol from a particular company for a period of five years. Obviously it is not possible to make such a contract at a fixed price since no one knows what the price of oil will be next month, let alone over the next five years. It would be legally permissible to provide for price indexation but in practice very difficult to find a sufficiently flexible and comprehensive index. Often the problem is solved by providing that the price is to be the list price at the date of delivery. There have been at least 20 litigated cases arising out of such contracts over the last 35 years since owners of filling stations are often anxious to escape from one petrol company into the arms of another but in none of these cases has it been argued that the price agreement is invalid.

One explanation for this would be that the buyer is protected in such cases by the requirement to pay the list price since this is the price that is being charged to all filling stations tied to that particular company and if a company were to treat all of its outlets badly, then those which were approaching renewal date would switch to another supplier. If this is right then a seller who agrees to sell at list price at date of delivery and who does not in fact have a price list may be in a different position. It would be possible to say that unilateral price-fixing is only adequately certain where it contains some objective element.

However, in *May and Butcher Ltd. v. R.* (1934)[1] Lord Dunedin said:

4-05

'With regard to price it is a perfectly good contract to say that the price is to be settled by the buyer.'

---

[1] [1934] 2 K.B. 17n.

In *Lombard Tricity Finance Ltd. v. Paton* (1989)[2] this was assumed to be correct by the Court of Appeal and applied to a contract which entitled a lender to change the interest rate unilaterally.

Rather than leave the price to be fixed by one party, the parties may agree that the price shall be fixed by agreement between them later. This is a common but potentially dangerous course. There is no problem if the parties do agree on a price but difficulties arise if they do not. It might be thought that in that case s. 8(2) would apply and a reasonable price would be due. However, in *May and Butcher v. R* (1934)[3] the House of Lords held otherwise. In that case there was a contract for the sale of tentage at a price to be agreed between the parties. The parties failed to agree and the House of Lords held that there was no contract. The argument which was accepted was that s. 8(2) only applied where there was no agreement as to the price so that its operation was excluded where the parties had provided a mechanism for fixing a price which had not worked. This decision had never been overruled and is still in theory binding. Nevertheless, the courts have not always followed it.

In *Foley v. Classique Coaches* (1934)[4] the plaintiffs sold land to the defendants who agreed as part of the same contract to buy all their petrol from the plaintiffs 'at a price to be agreed between the parties in writing and from time to time'. The transfer of the land was completed and the defendants later argued that the agreement to buy the petrol was not binding as the price was uncertain. This argument was rejected by the Court of Appeal. One can see a number of possible factors influencing this decision. The agreement to buy the petrol was only part, and a relatively small part, of the whole agreement; the rest of the agreement had been performed; the defendants had got the land and it is reasonable to think that their undertaking to buy petrol made them more attractive purchasers to the plaintiff so that they got a better price. The court also attached importance to a clause in the contract providing for disputes to be referred to arbitration though the general principle is that an arbitrator ought to reach exactly the same decision as the judge.

4-06 These two cases reflect a tension which exists throughout the law of contract. On the one hand judges feel that the parties should take care in the formulation of their agreements, employ competent lawyers and leave no loose ends; on the other hand, there is a feeling that the law should seek to serve the realities of commercial life and if there is a deal there should be a contract. Probably no judge holds in its extreme form

---

2   [1989] 1 All E.R. 918. See also *Shell UK Ltd. v. Lostock Garage* [1976] 1 W.L.R. 1187 where the question went by default.
3   [1934] 2 K.B. 17n.
4   [1934] 2 K.B. 1.

either view, but clearly some lean more to one side than to the other. Two recent cases from the general law of contract suggest that at the moment at least, the pendulum has swung in favour of the second view. In *Beer v. Bowden* (1981)[5] there was a lease for 14 years. The lease provided that the rent should be £1,250 a year for the first five years and thereafter:

'... such rent as shall be agreed between the landlords and the tenant ... and in any case ... not less than the yearly rental of £1,250.'

The contract provided no machinery for fixing the rent if the parties did not agree after the first five years and the tenant argued that he was entitled to stay for the full term at £1,250 a year. The Court of Appeal rejected this argument. It said that the purpose of the minimum rent provision was to cover the situation where rents generally fell and that it did not indicate that if there was no agreement the rent should stay at £1,250. The court considered that the parties had intended to agree that the rent should be a reasonable one. (It is important to note that in this case the tenant did not argue that the whole contract was invalid for uncertainty since the last thing he wished to do was to abandon the lease.)

The case suggests that the provision of defective machinery for reaching agreement is not inconsistent with an inference that the parties intend a reasonable price. This view is strongly reinforced by the decision of the House of Lords in *Sudbrook Trading Estate v. Eggleton* (1982)[6]. In that case there was a lease with an option for the tenant to buy the landlord's interest at a price to be agreed. The lease, which was clearly professionally drawn up, contained a provision that if the parties did not agree on the price it was to be fixed by two valuers, one to be appointed by either side. The lease did not provide for what was to happen if the valuers were not appointed. The tenant sought to exercise the option; the landlord by this time did not wish to sell, refused to appoint its valuer and argued that there was no binding contract. There was an unbroken series of cases for over a hundred years accepting this argument but the House of Lords rejected it. Their view was that in substance the parties clearly intended to agree on a reasonable price. This was reinforced by the provision for the appointment of valuers since they are professional people, who would be bound to apply professional and therefore reasonable standards. It followed that the agreement was clear and should not fail simply because the parties had provided defective machinery for carrying it out. If necessary the court could provide a means for discovering a reasonable price.

There is therefore a good chance that a court will hold where the parties do not agree that they intended the price to be a reasonable one.

---

5   [1981] 1 W.L.R. 522; [1981] 1 All E.R. 1071.
6   [1982] 3 All E.R. 1; [1983] 1 A.C. 444.

This is particularly likely where the goods have actually been delivered and accepted by the buyer. Nevertheless, it remains imprudent for the parties to make such an agreement granted that courts sometimes hold such agreements to be inadequately certain. These dangers can be avoided entirely by providing machinery for dealing with those cases where later agreement proves impossible or by simply providing that the price 'shall be such as the parties may later agree or in default of agreement a reasonable price'.

5 FIXING THE PRICE BY THIRD PARTY VALUATION

4-07   This is dealt with by s. 9 of the Sale of Goods Act 1979 which is set out above. The provisions are reasonably straightforward. Price fixing by third party valuation is valid but dependent on the third party actually undertaking the valuation. If one party prevents the valuation he or she is said to be liable to an action. Presumably it would be the seller who would usually prevent the valuation by not making the goods available. It is worth noting that the result of such obstruction by the seller is not a contract to sell at a reasonable price as is the case where the goods are delivered and no valuation takes place, but an action for damages. This may not make much difference in practice since what the buyer has been deprived of is the chance to purchase the goods at the price the valuer would have fixed and a court would almost certainly hold this to be the same as a reasonable price. (In many cases the buyer will not in fact recover substantial damages. This will become clearer after reading Chapter 10.)

An important question is what, if anything, sellers can do if they think the valuation too low, or what buyers can do if they think it is too high. No doubt the valuation is not binding if it can be shown that the valuer was fraudulently acting in concert with the other party. Apart from this case it would seem that it is binding as between seller and buyer. However, the party who is disappointed with the valuation will have an action against the valuer if it can be shown that the valuation was negligent. This was clearly accepted by the House of Lords in *Arenson v. Casson* (1977)[7], a case involving the sale of shares in a private company at a price fixed by valuation. In order to show that a valuation was negligent, it is not sufficient to show that other valuers would have reached a different figure. It must be shown that the figure produced was one that no reasonably competent valuer could have arrived at.

---

[7]   [1977] A.C. 747.

6 PRICE FLUCTUATIONS

If the contract is to run over a long period, a price which appears   **4-08**
sensible at the time the contract is made may come to seem quite
inappropriate later on. Two questions arise in this context. The first
concerns the steps the parties can take to provide for economic or market
fluctuations; the second is whether the law will intervene to relieve a
party who has entered into a fixed price contract which has been
overtaken by massive inflation (or indeed deflation).

We have already seen that the parties may, at least in some cases,
deal with price fluctuations by allowing one party to vary the price,
but clearly in many cases such an arrangement will not be acceptable
to the other party involved. The parties may agree to re-negotiate
prices from time to time but apart from the difficulties which have
already been pointed out, an endless cycle of re-negotiation may not be
commercially sensible.

It may therefore be desirable to provide a more structured solution
either by linking the price to an index or by providing a formula for
measuring increases or decreases in costs. At one time it was thought,
because of some remarks by Denning LJ in *Treseder - Griffin v. Cooperative
Insurance Society Ltd.* (1956)[8], that such attempts might be contrary to
public policy. The argument was that resistance to inflation demanded
unwavering allegiance to nominalism, the principle that a pound is a
pound is a pound. It is true that many economists think that systems in
which all wages are indexed to the cost of living fuel inflation since wage
increases filter fairly quickly back into the cost of living so that the
increases feed on themselves and multiply. However, it is quite a
different matter to forbid individuals to recognise the realities of
inflation and guard against it and this was recognised in the case of
Multiservice Bookbinding v. Marden (1979)[9] where an English mortgage in
which the capital repayments and interest were tied to the Swiss franc
was held to be valid.

Granted that provision against cost fluctuations in a long term   **4-09**
contract is permissible, how should it best be done? The most extensive
experience is in relation to construction contracts where two systems
have emerged. One is to take a baseline price and permit additions (and
reductions) because of prescribed increases (or decreases) in cost. In
principle this should produce a fair result but there are serious practical
difficulties in defining which cost increases can be passed on and to

---

8   [1956] 2 Q.B. 127.
9   [1979] Ch. 84.

what extent, especially as material and labour costs are not spread evenly over the life of the contract. This solution tends to produce complex formulae and much scope for dispute.

The other system is for the basic price to be indexed. In the building industry there are appropriate indices which are independent and regularly published. This produces a simple calculation and it may be assumed that in the long run occasional minor roughnesses even themselves out. However, this system does depend on the existence of an appropriate index. It would not be sensible, for example, to link sales of oil to the Retail Price Index since that may be going up when the price of oil is coming down. It would probably not make sense to tie petrol prices at the pump to OPEC posted prices or prices on the Rotterdam spot market since the first may be too stable and the latter too volatile to produce a sensible result. To pursue the index solution therefore requires the most careful examination of whether or not the index under consideration is appropriate.

4-10   Earlier a question was proposed as to whether English law would relieve a party who had entered into a fixed price contract which was overtaken by later events. In general the answer is that it will not and indeed there is only one case which contradicts that rule. This was the decision of the Court of Appeal in the striking case of *Staffordshire Area Health Authority v. South Staffordshire Waterworks* (1978)[10]. In this case the defendant entered into a contract in 1929 to supply water to the plaintiffs. The contract provided that 'at all times hereafter' the hospital was to receive 5,000 gallons of water a day free and all the additional water it required at the rate of 7 old pence (2.9 new pence) per 1,000 gallons. (This rate was about 70% of the then market rate.) By 1975 the market rate was 45p per 1,000 gallons. The Court of Appeal held that the defendants were entitled to give notice to terminate the agreement.

A number of observations may be made about the case. First, the termination came 46 years after the contract was made and the market price was then some 16 times the contract price (depending on what arithmetical allowance is made for the free gallons). In any view, therefore, the facts were strong and are unlikely to recur often. Secondly, only one of the judges (Lord Denning MR) explicitly based his decision on the effects of inflation; the other two judges purported to decide the case by reading the words 'at all times hereafter' as controlling the price only so long as the agreement continued and not as referring to its duration. It is difficult to believe, however, that they ignored the actual situation in arriving at this somewhat strange construction of the agreement.

---

[10]   [1978] 3 All E.R. 769; [1978] 1 W.L.R. 1387.

CHAPTER 5

DELIVERY AND PAYMENT

1 INTRODUCTION

Section 27 of the Sale of Goods Act 1979 provides:

5-01

'It is the duty of the seller to deliver the goods and of the buyer to accept and pay for them in accordance with the terms of the contract of sale.'

Section 28 states:

'Unless otherwise agreed, delivery of the goods and payment of the price are concurrent conditions, that is to say, the seller must be ready and willing to give possession of the goods to the buyer in exchange for the price and the buyer must be ready and willing to pay the price in exchange for possession of the goods.'

This chapter considers the legal problems arising from the duty of the seller to deliver the goods and of the buyer to accept and pay for them. It will discuss first the problems relating to payment and the relationship between payment and delivery, then the rules about delivery and finally the buyer's duty of acceptance.

2 PAYMENT

Section 28 states that, unless otherwise agreed, payment and delivery are concurrent conditions. This means that they should take place at the same time. Obviously, the parties may have agreed expressly or by implication that payment is to precede delivery or the other way round and this is extremely common. In practice payment and delivery cannot take place simultaneously without the willing co-operation of both parties and this means, as the second half of s. 28 makes clear, that the seller who complains that the buyer has not paid must show that he or she was ready and willing to deliver and conversely a buyer who complains of the seller's failure to deliver must show that he or she was ready and willing to pay the price. In practice this is often done by tendering the goods or the price respectively.

5-02

It is worth examining in a little more detail the position where the parties agree that payment is to precede delivery or vice versa. In commercial sales it is often agreed that goods will be delivered on usual trade terms, such as payment within 30 days or payment within 30 days of receipt of invoice. The effect of such an agreement is that the seller must deliver first and cannot subsequently have a change of mind and insist on payment on delivery. This would be so even if there were grounds for thinking that the buyer might not be able to pay. (It is arguably a defect in English law that, unlike some other systems, once the contract is under way there is no right to require convincing assurances that the other party can and will perform[1].) A seller in this position has in effect to gamble on whether any information about the buyer's inability to pay turns out to be true since the loss from delivering goods to a buyer who cannot pay for them will usually be greater than any liability in damages that might be incurred for non-delivery.

For the same reason a seller cannot refuse to deliver because the buyer has been late in paying on an earlier contract. Sellers often think they are entitled to do this and frequently do but it is clear that this is wrong. In *Total Oil v. Thompson* (1972)[2] a petrol company entered into a typical contract to supply petrol to a filling station. The contract provided for delivery on credit terms but the filling station owner turned out to be a bad payer and the petrol company attempted to change to a cash on delivery basis. It was held that they were not entitled to do this. A seller is of course entitled to change the payment terms in respect of future contracts.

5-03   It may be agreed that the buyer is to pay in advance. This often happens in international sales where the buyer agrees to pay by banker's letter of credit. In this case it is clear that the seller's obligation to deliver is conditional on the buyer having opened a letter of credit which complies with the terms of the contract. So in *W J Alan Co. Ltd. v. El Nasr Export and Import Co.* (1972)[3] there was a contract for the sale of coffee beans and the buyer agreed to open a credit in Kenyan shillings. In fact, the credit opened was in pounds sterling, though for the correct amount at the then prevailing rate of exchange. It was held that the seller's obligation to deliver (indeed to ship) the goods was conditional on the buyer opening a credit in Kenyan shillings.

Questions may arise about the form of payment. The starting point is that in the absence of contrary agreement the seller is entitled to be paid in cash but, of course, the parties are free to make other agreements.

In many cases it would be relatively easy to infer that payment by cheque was acceptable. Usually payment by cheque is said only to amount to a conditional discharge, that is the buyer is only discharged when the cheque is paid. This means that if the buyer's cheque bounces,

---

[1]   *cf.* Uniform Commercial Code 2.609.
[2]   [1972] 1 Q.B. 318.
[3]   [1972] 2 Q.B. 189.

the seller has a choice either to sue on the cheque or on the underlying transaction of sale. In the same way it has been held that a buyer who pays by banker's letter of credit is only conditionally discharged by the opening of the credit. So in *E D F Man Ltd. v. Nigerian Sweets and Confectionery Co. Ltd.* (1977)[4] the buyer had arranged a credit with a bank which went into liquidation before paying the seller. It was held that the buyer was liable for the price.

In international sales the price may be expressed in a foreign currency. In this situation it is vital to distinguish between the money of account and the money of payment. The money of account is the currency which measures the extent of the buyer's obligation; the money of payment is the currency in which payment is actually to be made. The two may be, but need not be, the same. The distinction is, of course, crucial in the case of fluctuations in currency value between the date of the contract and the date of payment. So it is the practice of the Rotterdam spot market in oil for all transactions to be in US dollars even though, as will often be the case, neither buyer nor seller is American. In such a market which is highly international, there are powerful arguments of convenience for all transactions being measured in a single currency[5].

3 DELIVERY

The first thing to say about 'delivery' is that the word bears a   5-04
meaning in the Sale of Goods Act 1979 quite different from its colloquial meaning. If I say that a grocer will deliver this would usually be taken to mean that the groceries will be brought to the house of a customer. In the Sale of Goods Act the word does not have any necessary connotation of taking the goods to the customer and refers simply to the seller's obligation to hand the goods over. In the basic case the seller performs his or her obligations by making the goods available to the buyer at his or her (the seller's) place of business.

It is undoubtedly prudent for the parties to spend some time thinking about delivery and well drafted conditions of sale or purchase contain provisions which deal with such questions as whether the customer is to collect the goods 'ex works' and if so whether the goods will be packed and whether labour will be available to help with loading. In many cases sellers may quote a price which includes carriage and in this event it is desirable to fix the destination and whether the price includes unloading and positioning or installation.

---

4   [1977] 2 Lloyds Rep. 50.
5   See Dicey and Morris on *The Conflict of Laws* (11th edn 1987) pp. 1441-2.

The Act provides an answer to some of these questions which applies in the absence of contrary agreement. In other cases the parties may use shorthand expressions like 'fob Felixstowe' or 'cif Hamburg' to which the courts have attached a body of meaning arising out of scores of litigated cases.

The meaning of delivery

5-05   Section 61(1) of the Sale of Goods Act 1979 states that delivery means 'voluntary transfer of possession from one person to another'. This is slightly misleading as it suggests that delivery necessarily involves the seller handing the goods to the buyer. Although the typical case is undoubtedly that of the seller making the goods available to the buyer at the place and time set out in the contract, there are many cases where this does not happen.

In some cases the buyer will already have been in possession of the goods. A typical example would be where goods were being acquired on hire-purchase and the customer exercised an option to buy the goods at the end of the period of hire. It would be absurd to require formal delivery and re-delivery of the goods. They are sufficiently delivered to the buyer in this case because there is a change in the capacity in which the goods are possessed.

Conversely the goods may be delivered even though the seller stays in possession if the capacity in which he or she is in possession changes. An example would be the practical position of the dealer in the standard hire-purchase car triangle (see Chapter 2). The dealer sells the car to the finance company but the car is never physically transferred to the finance company. It goes straight from dealer to customer. Physical transfer to the customer is a sufficient delivery to the finance company because the customer has only received possession because of a contract which recognises that the finance company is the owner of the car[6].

In some cases it may be sufficient to transfer the means of control. So delivery of a car may be made by transfer of the keys, and delivery of goods in a warehouse in the same way. This last example is very old and was discussed by Roman lawyers. It is sometimes called a symbolic delivery but at least for classical Roman law delivery of the key at the warehouse was required and this strongly suggests that control was the test[7].

---

[6]   This is easy enough to say in the standard situation where there are no complications. It has caused considerable difficulty where the underlying transactions are illegal. *Belvoir Finance Co. Ltd. v. Stapleton* [1971] 1 Q.B. 210, [1970] 3 All E.R. 664.

[7]   See De Zulueta, *Digest 41, 1* and 2 p. 54 discussing D41-1-9.6.

Section 29(4) of the Sale of Goods Act 1979 deals with the case of   **5-06**
goods which are in the possession of a third party. It provides:

> 'Where the goods at the time of sale are in the possession of a third
> person, there is no delivery by seller to buyer unless and until the
> third person acknowledges to the buyer that he holds the goods on
> his behalf; nothing in this section affects the operation of the issue or
> transfer of any document of title to the goods.'

The most common example of this would be where the seller had
put the goods into the hands of someone whose business it is to store
other people's goods, such as a warehouseman. Obviously, the seller
could tell the warehouseman to deliver the goods to the buyer but the
buyer might wish to leave the goods in the hands of the warehouseman.
Again, it would be absurd to require a formal delivery and redelivery
but here agreement between seller and buyer will not be sufficient to
effect delivery. The common practice is for the seller to give the buyer a
delivery order, that is a document instructing the warehouseman to
deliver to the buyer. The buyer can present this to the warehouseman
and ask that the goods be kept on his or her (the buyer's) behalf.
Delivery takes place when the warehouseman recognises that the buyer
is the person now entitled to the goods (this is technically known as an
'attornment').

This rule does not apply, as s. 29(4) of the 1979 Act states, where
there is a document of title involved. The notion of a document of title is
quite a difficult one and can best be explained by considering the most
important example, a bill of lading. A bill of lading is the document
issued by the master of a ship to a person who puts goods on board the
ship for carriage. The bill has a number of functions. It operates as
evidence of the terms on which the goods are to be carried and also as a
receipt for the goods. In the days of sail, goods might be put on board a
ship for carriage and the bill of lading sent ahead by a faster ship. The
practice grew up of dealing in the bills of lading and by the late 18th
century the courts had come to recognise the bill of lading as having a
third function of being a document of title to the goods on board ship. So
if the owners of goods put them on a ship and received a bill of lading
made out to themselves or 'to order', they could endorse the bill by
writing on its face a direction to deliver the goods to someone else and
that would transfer to that person the right to receive them from the
ship's master. In other words the shipowner is required to deliver to
whoever holds a bill of lading properly endorsed. In the case of
commodity cargoes where trading is very active, the goods may be
transferred many times while they are on the high seas.

The principal difference between the warehouseman and the ship's   **5-07**
master is that because the bill of lading is a document of title the transfer

is effective at once without the need for any attornment. In some cases it is not possible to transfer the bill of lading, for instance, because only part of the goods covered by the bill of lading is being sold. In this situation the seller may issue a delivery order addressed to the master but since the delivery order is not a document of title, delivery will not be effective until the master attorns.

Finally, delivery to a carrier may be a delivery to the buyer. This is dealt with by s. 32 which provides:

'(1) Where, in pursuance of a contract of sale, the seller is authorised or required to send the goods to the buyer, delivery of the goods to a carrier (whether named by the buyer or not) for the purpose of transmission to the buyer is *prima facie* deemed to be a delivery of the goods to the buyer.

(2) Unless otherwise authorised by the buyer, the seller must make such contract with the carrier on behalf of the buyer as may be reasonable having regard to the nature of the goods and the other circumstances of the case; and if the seller omits to do so, and the goods are lost or damaged in the course of transit, the buyer may decline to treat the delivery to the carrier as a delivery to himself or may hold the seller responsible in damages.

(3) Unless otherwise agreed, where goods are sent by the seller to the buyer by a route involving sea transit, under circumstances in which it is usual to insure, the seller must give such notice to the buyer as may enable him to insure during their sea transit; and if the seller fails to do so, the goods are at his risk during such sea transit.'

It should be emphasised that the rule that delivery to the carrier is delivery to the buyer is only a *prima facie* rule and can be rebutted by evidence of a contrary intention. So in the case of sea carriage if the seller takes the bill of lading to his or her own order as would usually be the case (so as to reserve a right of disposal, see Chapter 6) then this is evidence of a contrary intention. Further, if the seller sends the goods off in his or her own lorry this will not be delivery to a carrier for this purpose, nor probably if the carrier is an associated company.

5-08   One of the consequences of the rule that delivery to the carrier is delivery to the buyer may be that as between seller and buyer the 'risk' of accidental damage to the goods in transit will fall on the buyer. (This is discussed more fully in Chapter 7.) However, this possibility is qualified by s. 32(2) and (3) since if the seller fails to make a reasonable contract of carriage or, in the case of sea carriage to give notice enabling the buyer to insure, the risk will fall back on him or her. (In cif contracts, the most important form of export sale, it is part of the seller's obligations to insure.)

In *Young v. Hobson* (1949)[8] electrical engines were sold on for terms (that is free on rail - the seller's price covers the cost of getting the goods 'on rail'). The seller made a contract with the railway under which the goods were carried at the owner's risk when he could have made a contract for them to be carried at the carrier's risk at the same price, subject to an inspection by the railway. This was held not to have been a reasonable contract to have made.

Place of delivery

In many cases the parties will expressly agree the place of delivery or it will be a reasonable inference from the rest of their agreement that they must have intended a particular place.   5-09

If there is no express or implied agreement then the position is governed by s. 29(2) which provides:

> 'The place of delivery is the seller's place of business if he has one, and if not, his residence; except that, if the contract is for the sale of specific goods, which to the knowledge of the parties when the contract is made are in some other place, then that place is the place of delivery.'

This reflects the general position that in the absence of contrary agreement it is for the buyer to collect the goods but the language is very much that of 1893 rather than 1979 reflecting the fact that the 1979 Act was simply a tidying up operation. The language assumes that the seller has only one place of business which will very often not be the case today. Presumably, where the seller has several places of business the court will look at all the surrounding circumstances to see which of the seller's places of business is most appropriate.

Time of delivery

It is very common, particularly in commercial contracts, for the parties expressly to agree the date for delivery. This may be done either by selecting a particular calendar date, for example 1 May 1996, or by reference to a length of time, such as six weeks from receipt of order. In this respect it is worth noting that the law has a number of presumptions about the meaning of various time expressions, so that a year *prima facie* means any period of 12 consecutive months; a month means a calendar month; a week means a period of seven consecutive days and a day means the period from midnight to midnight (the law in general taking no account of parts of a day).   5-10

---

[8]   (1949) 65 T.L.R. 365.

The parties might agree that delivery is to be on request. This could happen, for instance, where the buyer can see the need for considerable volume over a period of time and does not wish to risk having to buy at short notice. If the buyer lacks storage facilities he or she may leave the goods with the seller and call them up as required. A typical example might be a builder who is working on a housing estate and can see how many bricks, doors, stairs, etc. will be needed but does not want to store them for long periods on site. In this situation the seller must deliver within a reasonable time from receiving the request and since the goods should have been set on one side, a reasonable time would be short.

The parties may completely fail to fix a date. The position will then be governed by s. 29(3) of the Sale of Goods Act 1979 which provides:

> 'Where under the contract of sale the seller is bound to send the goods to the buyer, but no time for sending them is fixed, the seller is bound to send them within a reasonable time.'

Although this sub-section only deals expressly with the case where the seller is bound to send the goods to the buyer, it is assumed that the same rule applies where the seller has to make the goods available for collection by the buyer. What is a reasonable time clearly depends on all the relevant circumstances. If the goods are in stock delivery should usually be possible within a few days; clearly if goods have to be made up to special requirements or ordered from another supplier or the manufacturer, a longer period will be reasonable.

Effect of late delivery

5-11　　　It is normally a breach of contract for the seller to deliver late[9]. The major exception to this rule would be where the contract gives some excuse for late delivery such as a *force majeure* clause. The buyer is entitled to damages to compensate for the loss suffered due to late delivery (see Chapter 10). In many cases, however, the buyer will not be able to show that any significant loss has been suffered as a result of the delay and the damages will only be nominal.

In some cases the buyer will be entitled to reject on late delivery, depending on whether 'time is of the essence'. This is one of those legal expressions which are widely known and frequently misunderstood. As far as the recovery of damages is concerned it does not matter at all whether time is of the essence, though curiously enough the House of

---

[9]　It may also be a breach of contract to tender delivery early. See *Bowes v. Shand* (1877) 2 App. Cas. 455 where the contract called for rice shipped during the months of March and/or April. The seller tendered rice shipped in February and the buyer was held entitled to reject. In cases of this kind the date of shipment is treated as part of the 'description' of the goods (see Chapter 8).

Lords did not finally decide this until *Rainieri v. Miles* (1981)[10]. For this purpose the only question is whether late performance was a breach of contract. However if, but only if, time is of the essence a late delivery can be rejected. Time can be of the essence for three reasons.

The first is that the contract expressly says so. In practice it often **5-12** contains a statement that time is (or alternatively is not) of the essence. Indeed one would expect well drafted conditions of purchase to make time of delivery of the essence while standard conditions of sale often say that the seller will do his or her best to deliver on time but does not give a guarantee to do so.

The second is that the court characterises the contract as one where time is inherently of the essence. This is essentially a two-stage process. In the first stage the court will consider whether the contract is of a kind where prompt performance is usually essential. So, for instance, prompt completion of a building contract is not usually imperative and indeed seems seldom to be achieved. The second stage is to consider whether there are particular circumstances which justify departure from the usual classification. So if the contract is to build a stadium for the next Olympics, it would probably be easy to persuade the court that it was important to complete the stadium before the beginning of the games. Applying this approach courts have consistently held that the time of delivery is normally of the essence in commercial sales.

The third possibility is that although time is not initially of the essence, the buyer may 'make' time of the essence. What this slightly misleading expression means is that if the seller does not deliver on time, a buyer may call on him or her to deliver within a reasonable time on pain of having the goods rejected if this does not happen. Provided the court later agrees with the buyer's assessment of what was a reasonable further time of delivery such a notice will be effective.

It is important to emphasise that if time is of the essence, buyers can **5-13** reject late delivery without any proof that in the particular case any real loss has been suffered. So, in a commercial contract of sale if delivery is due on 1 January, buyers would usually be entitled to reject delivery on 2 January. This means that if the buyers no longer want the goods, for instance because the market has moved against them, they can escape from the contract.

Buyers are not, of course, obliged to reject late delivery and indeed will often have little commercial alternative but to accept the goods because they are needed and not readily obtainable elsewhere. There is an important practical difference here between a buyer who purchases goods for resale and one who purchases goods for use. A buyer who

---

10   [1981] A.C. 1050.

accepts late delivery of the goods waives any right to reject for late delivery but does not waive the right to damages.

It may happen that the seller tells the buyer that the goods are going to be late but underestimates the extent of the delay. The difficulties that this may produce are well illustrated by the case of *Charles Rickards Ltd. v. Oppenheim* (1950)[11]. In this case, the plaintiff agreed to supply a Rolls Royce chassis for the defendant to be made by 20 March 1948. It was not ready by 20 March but the defendant continued to press for delivery. However, by June the defendant had lost patience with the plaintiff and on 29 June said that delivery could not be accepted after 25 July. The plaintiff did not tender delivery until 18 October and sued for damages for non-acceptance. The action failed. The correct analysis of this would seem to be that time was originally of the essence, that the defendant waived the right to reject by continuing to call for delivery but made time of the essence once more by the notice of 29 June.

Rules as to quantity delivered

5-14

Section 30 of the Sale of Goods Act 1979 contains a number of rules which deal with problems which arise where the seller delivers the wrong quantity. The basic rule is that the buyer is entitled to reject if the seller fails to deliver exactly the right quantity. Section 30(1) deals with the simplest case and provides:

'Where the seller delivers to the buyer a quantity of goods less than he contracted to sell, the buyer may reject them, but if the buyer accepts the goods so delivered he must pay for them at the contract rate.'

At first sight it seems obvious that the buyer is not bound to accept short delivery but there is an important practical consequence of this rule and the rule that the seller cannot deliver in instalments unless the contract expressly provides for delivery in that manner. It follows that if the seller delivers part of the goods and says that the balance is following, the buyer is entitled to reject. What happens in this situation if the buyer accepts the part delivery? It is probable that he or she has waived the right to reject but that this waiver is conditional on the seller honouring the undertaking to deliver the balance. If the seller fails to do so it seems probable that the buyer can reject after all. Of course, if he or she has meanwhile sold or consumed the part delivery, it will not be possible to reject since rejection depends on returning the goods.

---

[11] [1950] 1 K.B. 616.

When the seller tenders a partial delivery the buyer has a choice between rejecting the consignment and accepting the whole of the contract quantity. It is not possible to accept part of the delivery and reject the balance. Sections 30(2) and 30(3) deal with delivery of too much and provide:

'(2)   when the seller delivers to the buyer a quantity of goods larger than he contracted to sell, the buyer may accept the goods included in the contract and reject the rest, or he may reject the whole.

(3)   where the seller delivers to the buyer a quantity of goods larger than he contracted to sell and the buyer accepts the whole of the goods so delivered he must pay for them at the contract rate.'

It will be seen that buyers are entitled to reject not only if sellers   **5-15**
deliver too little but also if they deliver too much. This may appear surprising but it has the important practical consequence that a seller cannot force the buyer to select the right amount out of an excess delivery and this would be important in a case where the separation of the correct amount would be difficult and expensive. In this case, therefore, buyers have three alternatives: they may reject the whole delivery; they may accept the contract amount and reject the balance; or they may accept the whole delivery and pay *pro rata*.

Section 30(4) of the Sale of Goods Act 1979 provides:

'Where the seller delivers to the buyer the goods he contracted to sell mixed with goods of a different description not included in the contract, the buyer may accept the goods which are in accordance with the contract and reject the rest, or he may reject the whole.'

A good example of this rule in practice is the pre-Act case of *Levy v. Green* (1859)[12] where the buyer ordered crockery and the seller delivered the correct amount of the crockery ordered together with some more crockery of a different pattern. In this case the buyer again had three choices:

(a) to reject the whole delivery;

(b) to accept the contract delivery and reject the balance; or

(c) to accept the whole delivery.

It will be seen that this is very similar to the case of delivering too much; the only difference being that if the excess is accepted it must be paid for at a reasonable price rather than at the contract rate (since there is no contract rate for non contract goods). Many commentators have

---

[12]   (1859) 1 E&E 969.

thought that s. 30(4) was only aimed at the case of a delivery in full with an admixture of other goods. However, the courts have also applied it to a mixture of a short delivery of the contract goods together with other goods. So in *Ebrahim Dawood Ltd. v. Heath Ltd.* (1961)[13] there was a contract for the delivery of 50 tons of steel sheets of five different sizes 'equal tonnage per size'. Instead of delivering 10 tons of each of the five sizes the seller delivered 50 tons of one size. This was treated as being a mixture of 10 tons of the right size and 40 tons of the wrong size so that the buyer was entitled to accept the 10 tons and reject the balance.

It will be seen that the rules stated in s. 30(1)-(4) of the Sale of Goods Act 1979 impose a very strict duty on the seller to deliver the correct quantity of goods. It is, of course, open to the parties to modify this and this is expressly recognised by s. 30(5) which provides:

> 'This section is subject to any usage of trade, special agreement, or course of dealing between the parties.'

So a seller may be able to show that there is a settled practice between the parties that the buyer always accepts what is delivered or that there is a usage in the trade to that effect. That would require proof of previous dealings between the parties or of the practices of the particular trade to which the parties belong respectively.

5-16   It is clearly open to the parties to deal with the matter by the contract. There are a number of ways in which this might be done. It is common in commodity contracts for there to be an express tolerance, for example, 1,000 tons Western White Wheat, 5% more or less at the seller's option. In such a case any amount between 950 tons and 1,050 tons would be a contract amount but the rules in s. 30 would apply to deliveries of 949 or 1,051 tons. Another possibility would be that the contract was for the sale of a particular bulk, say 'all the sugar in my warehouse in Bristol, thought to be about 500 tonnes'. In this case there would be a binding contract even if there were 400 tonnes or 600 tonnes in the warehouse though if the figure of 500 had not been an honest estimate the seller might be liable for misrepresentation.

Section 30 is amended by s. 4 of the Sale and Supply of Goods Act 1994 which adds a new section (2A) which provides:

> '(2A)   A buyer who does not deal as consumer may not –
>
> (a)   where the seller delivers a quantity of goods less than he contracted to sell, reject the goods under subsection (1) above, or

---

[13]   [1961] 2 Lloyds Rep. 512.

(b)   where the seller delivers a quantity of goods larger than
                he contracted to sell, reject the whole under subsection (2)
                above,

if the shortfall or, as the case may be, excess is so slight that it would
be unreasonable for him to do so.'

So the buyer's right of rejection is now qualified in the case of non
consumer sales, where the shortfall or excess is so slight that it would be
unreasonable for the buyer to reject. It seems that there are two stages;
first the court decides that the shortfall (or excess) is slight. Secondly, it
decides that, in the circumstances, it would be unreasonable to allow the
buyer to reject.

Apart from this the only other qualification of the strictness of the   **5-17**
rules in s. 30 occurs where it is possible to invoke the legal maxim *de
minimis non curat lex* which may be roughly translated as the law takes
no account of very small matters. Undoubtedly, this principle can apply,
but for this purpose very small means very, very small. One of the few
examples is *Shipton Anderson v. Weil Brothers* (1912)[14] where the contract
was to sell 4,950 tons of wheat and the seller delivered an excess of 55
pounds. It was held that the buyer was not entitled to reject. The
discrepancy in this case was of the order of 0.0005% which is certainly
very small. All systems of measurement contain some margin of error
and it seems safe to say that a buyer cannot reject for a discrepancy
which is within the margin of error of the appropriate system. This
seems especially so where it is clear that if there is an error it is in the
buyer's favour (assuming as would usually be the case in such situations
the seller is claiming no more than the contract price). However, it also
seems clear that the scope for applying the *de minimis* principle in this
area is very limited.

Delivery by instalments

Section 31(1) of the Sale of Goods Act 1979 provides:

'Unless otherwise agreed, the buyer of goods is not bound to accept
delivery of them by instalments.'

The Act does not expressly say so but it must surely also be the case
that the buyer is not entitled to call on the seller to deliver by
instalments, unless otherwise agreed.

Of course, delivery by instalment is in practice very common and
indeed many contracts of sale could not be performed in any other way.

---

14   [1912] 1 K.B. 574.

The Act does not define instalment and there would be scope for argument as to whether a delivery was by instalment. Let us suppose for instance that a contractor building a motorway makes a contract for 1,000 tons of pre-coated chippings for immediate delivery and that there is no lorry which can be legally driven on the roads capable of carrying more than 100 tons. It will be implicit in the contract that at least 10 lorry loads will be necessary. If 10 lorries arrive simultaneously is that a delivery by instalments? One suspects that the answer is in the negative, but if that is right, what is the position if one of the lorries breaks down on the way to the site? It is thought that this is covered by s. 30(1) (see Rules as to quantity delivered) rather than by s. 31(1).

5-18   Where the parties decide on delivery by instalments there are a number of practical questions which ideally they ought to answer in the contract. A basic question is whether to opt for a fixed schedule of instalments or to allow the seller or the buyer options as to the timing and number of instalments. If there are to be fixed instalments then the number and intervals need to be fixed and the contract should say whether they are to be of equal size.

It seems desirable to say something here about defective performance of instalment contracts. (Remedies in general are more fully discussed in Chapter 10.) Either party can, of course, bring an action for damages for loss resulting from a defective performance in relation to one instalment. The critical question is whether faulty performance in relation to one instalment entitles a party to terminate the contract. In other words, can a seller refuse to deliver a second instalment because the buyer has not paid for the first one or, conversely, can the buyer treat the contract as at an end because the goods delivered under one instalment are faulty?

As has been stated, where there are a series of separate contracts it is not possible to refuse to perform a second contract because the other party failed to perform the first. This rule does not apply to a single contract performable in instalments even where the contract provides 'each delivery a separate contract' since the House of Lords held in *Smyth v. Bailey* (1940)[15] that these words did not actually operate to divide the contract up.

In the case of instalment contracts it is undoubtedly open to the parties explicitly to provide that defective performance by one party in relation to any one instalment entitles the other party either to terminate or at least to withhold performance until that defect is remedied. Even if the parties do not explicitly so provide, defective performance in relation

---

[15]   [1940] 3 All E.R. 60.

to one instalment may still have this effect because of s. 31(2) of the Sale of Goods Act 1979 which provides:

> 'Where there is a contract for the sale of goods to be delivered by stated instalments, which are to be separately paid for, and the seller makes defective deliveries in respect of one or more deliveries, or the buyer neglects or refuses to take delivery of or pay for one or more instalments, it is a question in each case depending on the terms of the contract and the circumstances of the case whether the breach of contract is a repudiation of the whole contract or whether it is a severable breach giving rise to a claim for compensation but not to treat the whole contract as repudiated.'

This sub-section does not expressly cover all the things which may go wrong with instalment contractors. For instance, it does not cover the case where the seller fails to make a delivery at all rather than making a defective delivery, nor does it cover the case where the instalments are not 'stated' but are at the buyer's or seller's option. Nevertheless, these situations seem also to be covered by the test laid down which is that everything turns on whether the conduct of the party in breach amounts to a repudiation by that party of his or her obligations under the contract. This concept is considered in more detail in Chapter 10 but for present purposes it can be said that it must be shown either that the contract breaker has expressly or implicitly stated that he or she does not intend to fulfil the contract or that the innocent party has been substantially deprived of what was contracted for. In practice the courts are very reluctant to treat defective performance in relation to a single instalment as passing this test. An accumulation of defects over several instalments may do so as in *Munro v. Meyer* (1930)[16] where there was a contract to buy 1500 tons of meat and bone meal, delivery at the rate of 125 tons a month. After more than half had been delivered the meal was discovered to be defective. It was held that the buyer was entitled to terminate and reject future deliveries. **5-19**

The case of *Regent OHG Aisenstadt v. Francesco of Jermyn Street* (1981)[17] revealed that there is a conflict between s. 30(1) and s. 31(2) of the 1979 Act. In this case the sellers were manufacturers of high class men's suits and contracted to sell 62 suits to the buyers who had an expensive retail outlet. Delivery was to be in instalments at the seller's option. The sellers in fact tendered the suits in five instalments. For reasons which had nothing to do with this contract the parties fell out and the buyers refused to accept delivery of any of the instalments. This was clearly a repudiation and the sellers would have been entitled to terminate. In fact the sellers did not do so and continued to tender the

---

[16] [1930] 2 K.B. 312.
[17] [1981] 3 All E.R. 327; [1988] 1 W.L.R. 321.

suits. Shortly before tendering the fourth instalment the sellers told the buyers that because a particular cloth was not available the delivery would be one suit short. This shortfall was not made up in the fifth and final delivery so that the sellers ended up by tendering 61 suits instead of 62. It was clear that if the contract had been for a single delivery of 62 suits the case would have been governed by s. 30(1) and the buyer would have been entitled to reject delivery which was one suit short. Equally clearly, however, the seller's conduct did not amount to repudiation within the test laid down by s. 31(2) for delivery by instalments. It was held that insofar as there was a conflict between ss. 30(1) and 31(2) the latter must prevail and that the buyer was accordingly not entitled to reject.

4 ACCEPTANCE

5-20   Section 27 of the Sale of Goods Act 1979, quoted above, talks of the seller's duty to deliver the goods and the buyer's duty to accept. At first sight one might think that the buyer's duty to accept is the converse of the seller's duty to deliver, that is the duty to take delivery. However, it is quite clear that although acceptance and taking delivery are connected they are not the same thing. In fact 'acceptance' is a sophisticated and difficult notion.

Section 35(1) provides:

'The buyer is deemed to have accepted the goods when he intimates to the seller that he has accepted them, or (except where section 34 above otherwise provides) when the goods have been delivered to him and he does any act in relation to them which is inconsistent with the ownership of the seller, or when after the lapse of a reasonable time he reclaims the goods without intimating to the seller that he has rejected them.'

This section does not so much define acceptance as explain when it happens. It is implicit in the section that acceptance is the abandonment by the buyer of any right to reject the goods. (This by no means involves the abandonment of any right to damages.) The buyer may be entitled to reject goods for a number of different reasons; for instance (as we have already seen) because the seller delivers too many or too few goods or, sometimes, delivers them late. Other grounds for rejection, such as defects in the goods, will be dealt with later.

Section 35 of the Act tells us that buyers can abandon the right to reject the goods, that is 'accept' them in a number of different ways. Before examining these it is worth noting that buyers cannot be under a duty to accept in this sense since they would be perfectly entitled to reject the goods in such cases. Buyers can only be under a duty to accept when they have no right to reject. In s. 27 therefore the word 'accept' must mean something different from what it means in s. 35, that is, something much closer to a duty to take delivery.

The reason for the elaboration of s. 35 is that in this area the law of **5-21**
sale appears to be slightly different from the general law of contract. The buyer's right of rejection is analogous to the right of an innocent party to terminate in certain circumstances for the other party's breach of contract. Under the general law of contract it is not usually possible to argue that a party has waived the right to terminate unless it can be shown that he or she knew the relevant facts which so entitled him or her but in the law of sale the buyer may lose the right to reject before knowing he or she had it. This is no doubt hard on the buyer but probably justified on balance by the desirability of not allowing commercial transactions to be upset too readily. So the buyer loses the right to reject not only by expressly accepting but also by failing to reject within a reasonable time or by doing an act which is inconsistent with the ownership of the seller, such as sub-selling.

A key question here is what is a 'reasonable time'. In *Bernstein v. Pamson Motors Ltd.* (1987)[18] the plaintiff sought to reject a new motor car whose engine seized up after he had owned it for three weeks and driven it only 140 miles. Rougier J held that the car was not of merchantable quality but that a reasonable time had elapsed and the right to reject had been lost. He took the view that the reasonableness of the time did not turn on whether the defect was quickly discoverable but on:

'What is a reasonable practical interval in commercial terms between a buyer receiving the goods and his ability to send them back, taking into consideration from his point of view the nature of the goods and their function, and from the point of view of the seller the commercial desirability of being able to close his ledger reasonably soon after the transaction is complete.'[19]

Although the buyer may lose the right to reject quite quickly it would be very harsh if the buyer lost the right to reject before there had been a chance to examine the goods, since in many cases the buyer will not be able to tell at the moment the goods are delivered that they are defective. So s. 34 of the 1979 Act provides:

'(1)   Where goods are delivered to the buyer, and he has not previously examined them, he is not deemed to have accepted them

---

18   [1987] 2 All E.R. 220.
19   This result can reasonably be described as less than self evident and it was widely criticised by consumer groups. There are many Canadian cases on the meaning of this section and some at least are perceptibly more generous to buyers. See Bridge, *Sale of Goods* (Butterworths, Canada, 1988) pp. 293-295.

until he has had a reasonable opportunity of examining them for the purpose of ascertaining whether they are in conformity with the contract.

(2)   Unless otherwise agreed, when the seller tenders delivery of goods to the buyer, he is bound on request to afford the buyer a reasonable opportunity of examining the goods for the purpose of ascertaining whether they are in conformity with the contract.'

5-22   It is important to note that s. 35 is made subject to s. 34 so that a buyer does not lose the right to reject by failing to do so within a reasonable time or by doing acts inconsistent with the seller's ownership if he or she has not had a reasonable opportunity of examination. Suppose, for instance, that A sells goods to B and B sub-sells the same goods to C and that B tells A to deliver the goods direct to C. The goods delivered by A are defective and C rejects them. If s. 35 stood alone B would not be able to reject because the sub-sale was inconsistent with A's ownership; however, the overriding effect of s. 34 means that B can reject in this situation because there has not been a reasonable opportunity to examine the goods. Of course, B will not be able to reject unless C has rejected since otherwise he or she will not be able to return the goods, but it is precisely C's rejection which is the event which will make B wish to reject.

Both s. 34 and s. 35 have been amended by the Sale and Supply of Goods Act 1994. Set out below are both the 1979 and 1994 versions, underlining the new words in the 1994 version and indicating deletions from the 1979 version by striking through in the text of the 1994 version:

'**34 Buyer's right of examining the goods**

(1) Where goods are delivered to the buyer, and he has not previously examined them, he is not deemed to have accepted them until he has had a reasonable opportunity of examining them for the purpose of ascertaining whether they are in conformity with the contract.

(2) Unless otherwise agreed, when the seller tenders delivery of the goods to the buyer, he is bound on request to afford the buyer a reasonable opportunity of examining the goods for the purpose of ascertaining whether they are in conformity with the contract.

34 Buyer's right of examining the goods

(1) Where goods are delivered to the buyer, and he has not previously examined them, he is not deemed to have accepted them until he has had a reasonable opportunity of examining them for the purpose of ascertaining whether they are in conformity with the contract.

(2) Unless otherwise agreed, when the seller tenders delivery of goods to the buyer, he is bound on request to afford the buyer a reasonable opportunity of examining the goods for the purpose of ascertaining whether they are in conformity with the contract, and, in the case of a contract for sale by sample, of comparing the bulk with the sample.

35 Acceptance

(1) The buyer is deemed to have accepted the goods when he intimates to the seller that he has accepted them, or (except where section 34 above otherwise provides) when the goods have been delivered to him and he does any act in relation to them which is inconsistent with the ownership of the seller, or when after the lapse of a reasonable time he retains the goods without intimating to the seller that he has rejected them.

35 Acceptance

(1) The buyer is deemed to have accepted the goods <u>when he intimates to the seller that he has accepted them, or (except where section 34 above otherwise provides) when the goods have been delivered to him and he does any act in relation to them which is inconsistent with the ownership of the seller, or when after the lapse of a reasonable time he retains the gods without intimating to the seller that he has rejected them</u> subject to subsection (2) below –

<u>(a)</u> <u>when he intimates to the seller that he has accepted them, or</u>

<u>(b)</u> <u>when the goods have been delivered to him and he does any act in relation to them which is inconsistent with the ownership of the seller.</u>

<u>(2)</u> <u>Where goods are delivered to the buyer, and he has not previously examined them, he is not deemed to have accepted them under subsection (1) above until he has had a reasonable opportunity of examining them for the purpose -</u>

<u>(a)</u> <u>of ascertaining whether they are in conformity with the contract, and</u>

<u>(b)</u> <u>in the case of a contract for sale by sample, of comparing the bulk with the sample.</u>

<u>(3)</u> <u>Where the buyer deals as consumer or (in Scotland) the contract of sale is a consumer contract, the buyer cannot lose his right to rely on subsection (2) above by agreement, waiver or otherwise.</u>

<u>(4)</u> <u>The buyer is also deemed to have accepted the goods when after</u>

the lapse of a reasonable time he retains the goods without intimating to the seller that he has rejected them.

(5) The questions that are material in determining for the purposes of subsection (4) above whether a reasonable time has elapsed include whether the buyer has had a reasonable opportunity of examining the goods for the purpose mentioned in subsection (2) above.

(6) The buyer is not by virtue of this section deemed to have accepted the goods merely because -

(a) he asks for, or agrees to, their repair by or under an arrangement with the seller, or

(b) the goods are delivered to another under a sub-sale or other disposition.

(7) Where the contract is for the sale of goods making one or more commercial units, a buyer accepting any goods included in a unit is deemed to have accepted all the goods making the unit; and in this subsection "commercial unit" means a unit division of which would materially impair the value of the goods or the character of the unit.

'(2) Paragraph 10 of Schedule 1 below applies in relation to a contract made before 22 April 1967 or (in the application of this Act to Northern Ireland) 28 July 1967.

(2)(8) Paragraph 10 of Schedule 1 below applies in relation to a contract made before 22 April 1967 or (in the application of this Act to Northern Ireland) 28 July 1967.'

Under the 1994 version, all three of the grounds for acceptance are subject to the buyer's right to examine the goods. This is done by moving the right to examine the goods from s. 34(1) to s. 35(2) and by making acceptance under s. 35(1) subject to s. 35(2). So, even if the buyer tells the seller that he has accepted the goods, this is not binding until he has had a reasonable opportunity of examining them.

There are a number of other changes. Section 35(3) is important in view of the widespread practice of asking consumer buyers to sign acceptance notes. A consumer buyer will not lose his right to rely on his not having had a reasonable opportunity to examine the goods because the delivery man got him to sign a note of acceptance. It should be noted that it is the right to examine which cannot be lost by 'agreement, waiver or otherwise'. This does not mean that the right to reject cannot be lost by 'agreement, waiver or otherwise' once the right to examine has been exercised. So, if defective goods are delivered to a consumer buyer who examines them, decides that they are defective but decides to keep them, he will not later be able to say that he has not accepted them. However, this is also qualified by the change in s. 35(6). A reasonable buyer will often wish to give the seller a chance to make the goods work. A disincentive to doing this was that one might be advised that giving the seller a chance to repair was an acceptance, thereby preventing a later rejection of the goods if the repair was ineffective. This is now not the case.

Is *Bernstein v Pamson Motors Ltd* reversed by the 1994 Act? The wording in the latter part of s. 35(1) of the 1979 version now appears in s. 35(4) in the same terms. However, s. 35(4) is now qualified by s. 35(5) and it may be argued that this has had the effect of altering the notion of a reasonable time. However, the defect in *Bernstein v Pamson Motors* was one which could not have been discovered by any kind of examination. It was an internal defect in the engine which made it certain that the engine would seize up but could only be discovered when the engine in fact seized up. Although the decision in *Bernstein v Pamson Motors* has been widely criticised, it is far from clear that the Act has reversed it.

Instead of waiting for the seller to tender delivery and then refusing to accept, the buyer may announce in advance that he or she will not take the goods. Usually this will amount to an 'anticipatory breach' (discussed more fully in Chapter 10) and will entitle the seller to terminate the contract though he or she may choose instead to continue to tender the goods in the hope that the buyer will have a change of mind and take them.

A difficult problem arises where buyers announce in advance that they will not take the goods and later seek to argue that they would have been entitled to reject the goods in any case because they were defective.

5-23

The general rule in the law of contract is that a party who purports to terminate for a bad reason can usually justify the termination later by relying on a good reason which has only just been discovered. Of course, the buyer will often have great practical problems in establishing that the goods which the seller would have delivered would have been defective. This is probably the explanation of the difficult and controversial case of *British and Benningtons v. N W Cachar Tea* (1923)[20] where the buyer had contracted to buy tea to be delivered to a bonded warehouse in London. There was no express date for delivery and delivery was therefore due within a reasonable time. Before a reasonable time had elapsed the buyers said that they would not accept delivery. The ships carrying the tea had been diverted by the shipping controller and the buyers seem to have thought that this would prevent delivery within a reasonable time. (The buyer and the court took different views of what time would be reasonable.) The House of Lords held that the buyer had committed an anticipatory breach and that the seller could recover damages. The best explanation of this result seems to be that at the time of the buyer's rejection, the seller had not broken the contract and although he could not prove that he would certainly have delivered within a reasonable time, the buyer could not prove that the seller would not have delivered within a reasonable time. The position would be different if the seller had committed a breach of contract so that it could be said for certain that he would not be able to deliver within a reasonable time.

---

[20]   [1923] A.C. 48.

CHAPTER 6

OWNERSHIP

1 INTRODUCTION

The primary purpose of a contract for the sale of goods, is to transfer ownership of the goods from the seller to the buyer. This chapter deals with a series of problems which arise in this connection. The first involves the nature of the seller's obligations as to the transfer of ownership; the second concerns the moment at which ownership is transferred and the third, the circumstances in which a buyer may become owner of goods, even though the seller was not the owner.

6-01

It is necessary, first of all, to say something about terminology[1]. The Sale of Goods Act does not in general talk about ownership. It does talk a good deal about 'property' and 'title'. Both of these words can, for present purposes, be regarded as synonyms for ownership. The Act uses the word 'property', when dealing with the first two questions above and 'title' when dealing with the third. This is because the first two questions involve disputes between seller and buyer, whereas the third question involves a dispute between an owner who was not the seller, and the buyer. We shall also encounter the expression 'reservation of the right of disposal' which, despite appearances, also turns out to be another expression effectively meaning ownership. A distinction is sometimes drawn between the 'general property' and the 'special property'. Here the words 'general property' are being used to describe ownership and the words 'special property' to describe possession, that is physical control without the rights of ownership. So if I rent a television set for use in my home, the rental company has the general property (ownership) and I have the special property (possession).

2 THE SELLER'S DUTIES AS TO THE TRANSFER OF OWNERSHIP

The seller's duties are set out in s. 12 of the Act which provides:

6-02

'12 (1) In a contract of sale, other than one to which sub-section (3) below applies, there is an implied condition on the part of the seller

---

[1] Battersby and Preston, 35 M.L.R. 268.

that in the case of a sale he has a right to sell the goods, and in the case of an agreement to sell he will have such a right at the time when the property is to pass.

(2)   In a contract of sale, other than one to which sub-section (3) below applies, there is also an implied warranty that -

(a) the goods are free, and will remain free until the time when the property is to pass, from any charge or encumbrance not disclosed or known to the buyer before the contract is made, and

(b) the buyer will enjoy quiet possession of the goods except so far as it may be disturbed by the owner or other person entitled to the benefit of any charge or encumbrance so disclosed or known.'

It will be seen that these two sub-sections set out three separate obligations. Of these, by far the most important is that set out in s. 12(1), under which the seller undertakes that he or she has the right to sell the goods. It is important to note that the seller is in breach of this obligation, even though he or she believes that he or she is entitled to sell the goods and even though the buyer's enjoyment of the goods is never disturbed. Suppose, for instance, that X's goods are stolen by A, who sells them to B, who sells them to C, who sells them to D. In this situation X can claim the goods or their value from A, B, C or D. Obviously he cannot recover more than once but he has a completely free choice as to whom to sue. In practice, he would usually not sue the thief A because he has disappeared or spent the money. He is more likely to sue D, who still has the goods, unless B or C for some reason appear more attractive defendants (for example, because D has left the country). However, so far as the rights of the parties to the individual contracts of sale are concerned, it makes no difference who X sues or even that he sues no one. A is still in breach of his contract with B; B is in breach of his contract with C and C is in breach of his contract with D. What X has done may affect the amount of money, if any, that can be recovered in any of these actions, but not the existence of the obligation.

6-03   Section 12(1) talks about the right to sell and not about the transfer of ownership. There are cases where the seller has no right to sell, but does transfer ownership because it is one of the exceptional cases where a non-owner seller can make the buyer owner. In such cases, the seller will be in breach of s. 12(1). In most cases the seller will be entitled to sell, either because he or she is the owner or is the agent of the owner or because he or she will be able to acquire ownership before property is to pass (as will be the case with future goods). Perhaps surprisingly, it has been held that even though the seller is the owner, he or she may, in exceptional circumstances, not have a right to sell the goods. This is well illustrated by the leading case of *Niblett v. Confectioner's Materials* (1921)[2] where the plaintiffs bought tins of milk from the defendants. Some of the tins of milk were delivered bearing labels 'Nissly brand', which infringed the trademark of another manufacturer. That manufacturer persuaded the Customs and Excise to impound the tins and the plaintiffs had to remove and destroy the labels, before they could get the tins back. It was held that the defendants were in breach of s. 12(1) because they did not have the right to sell the tins in the condition in which they were, even though they owned them. This was clearly reasonable, as the plaintiffs had been left with a supply of unlabelled tins which would be difficult to dispose of.

To what remedy is the buyer entitled if the seller breaks his or her obligation under s. 12(1)?

The buyer can certainly recover, by way of damages, any loss which **6-04** he or she has suffered because of the breach. Further, the seller's obligation is stated to be a condition and as we shall see (Chapter 10), the buyer is generally entitled to reject the goods when there is a breach of condition. In practice, however, it will very seldom be possible to use this remedy because the buyer will not usually know until well after the goods have been delivered, that the seller has no right to sell.

In *Rowland v. Divall* (1923)[3] the Court of Appeal held that the buyer had a more extensive remedy. In that case, the defendant honestly bought a stolen car from the thief and sold it to the plaintiff, who was a car dealer, for £334. The plaintiff sold the car for £400. In due course, some four months after the sale by the defendant to the plaintiff, the car was repossessed by the police and returned to its true owner. Clearly on these facts, there was a breach of s. 12(1) and the plaintiff could have maintained a damages action, but in such an action it would have been necessary to take account not only of the plaintiff's loss, but also of any benefit he and his sub-buyer had received by having use of the car. The Court of Appeal held, however, that the plaintiff was not restricted to an action for damages, but could sue to recover the whole of the price. This was on the basis that there was a total failure of consideration; that is, that the buyer had received none of the benefit for which he had entered the contract, since the whole object of the transaction was that he should become the owner of the car.

---

2 [1921] 3 K.B. 387.
3 [1923] 2 K.B. 500.

It is important to note that the reasoning in *Rowland v. Divall* turns on the view that the whole object of the transaction is that the buyer becomes the owner of the goods. Accordingly, it does not matter that the buyer has never been dispossessed. Of course, he or she cannot have the price back and keep the goods, if he or she has them, but the situation may arise where the buyer does not have the goods, but has never been evicted by the true owner. Suppose, for instance that A steals a case of wine from X and sells it to B, who sells it to C, who drinks all the wine before the theft becomes apparent. It appears that C can recover the price in full from B, even though he has drunk the wine. This would not be so surprising if C had been sued by X, but as we have seen, X can, if he chooses, sue B. So on these facts B, who may be entirely innocent and honest, can be sued by both X and by C. Obviously this does not appear a fair result.

6-05   No English case has presented these facts, but *Rowland v. Divall* was carried a stage further in *Butterworth v. Kingsway Motors* (1954)[4]. Here X, who was in possession of a car under a hire-purchase agreement, sold it to Y before he had paid all the instalments. Y sold the car to Z, who sold it to the defendant, who sold it to the plaintiff. X meanwhile continued to pay the instalments. Several months later, the plaintiff discovered that the car was subject to a hire-purchase agreement and demanded the return of the price from the defendant. Eight days later, X paid the last instalment and exercised his option under the hire purchase contract to buy the car. The result of this was that the ownership of the car passed from the finance company to X and so on down the line to the plaintiff. It followed that the plaintiff was no longer at risk of being dispossessed but it was nevertheless held that he could recover the price. Later developments did not expunge the breach of s. 12(1), since the defendant had not had the right to sell at the time of the sale. It will be seen that the plaintiff, who had suffered no real loss, in effect received a windfall since his use of the car was entirely free.

It is interesting to ask what the position would have been if the plaintiff had demanded return of the price nine days later, that is, after X had paid the last instalment. In the Northern Ireland case of *West v. McBlain* (1950)[5] Sheil J thought that the buyer would still have been entitled to demand return of the price. This is logical, but it may be thought that it pushes logic one step too far. Certainly that was the view expressed by Pearson J in *Butterworth v. Kingsway Motors* in considering this possibility.

4   [1954] 1 W.L.R. 1286; [1954] 2 All E.R. 694.
5   [1950] N.I. 144.

A statutory exception to *Rowland v. Divall* has been created by s. 6(3) of the Torts (Interference with Goods) Act 1977. This deals with the situation where the goods have been improved by an innocent non-owner. If, on the facts of *Butterworth v. Kingsway Motors*, one of the parties in the chain had replaced the engine, then the plaintiff would have had to give credit for this enhancement of the car's value in his or her action for the price. It would not matter for this purpose whether the new engine was fitted by the defendant or by one of the previous owners, provided that the engine was fitted by someone, who at the time of fitting, believed that he or she was the owner.

Subsidiary obligations

In most cases, the buyer's protection against a seller who has a defective title to the goods, will be under s. 12(1). Section 12(2) provides two subsidiary obligations which cover situations which might not be covered by s. 12(1). Section 12(2) (a) deals with the case where the seller owns the goods, but has charged them in a way not disclosed to the buyer. A possible example would be if I were to sell you my watch which, unknown to you, is at the pawnbroker's. This is not likely to happen very often because most forms of borrowing against goods, in English practice, involve transferring ownership to the lender and will therefore fall, if at all, under s. 12(1). **6-06**

A good example of the operation of the warranty of quiet possession under s. 12(2) (b) is *Microbeads v. Vinhurst Road Markings* (1975)[6]. In this case the buyer found himself subject to a claim by a patentee of a patent affecting the goods. The patent had not in fact existed at the time the goods were sold and there was, accordingly, no breach of s. 12(1). The Court of Appeal held, however, that s. 12(2) covered the case where the patent was issued after the sale.

Section 12(2) states that the obligations contained in it are warranties and it follows that the buyer's only remedy, in the event of breach, is an action for damages.

Can the seller exclude his or her liability under s. 12?

In its 1893 version, s. 12 contained after the words 'in a contract of sale' the words 'unless the circumstances of the contract are such as to show a different intention'. This strongly suggested that the draughtsman contemplated the possibility that the contract might **6-07**

---

6   [1975] 1 All E.R. 529; [1975] 1 W.L.R. 218.

contain a clause excluding or qualifying the seller's duties under the section. Some commentators argued, on the other hand, that if transfer of ownership were, as held in *Rowland v. Divall*, the whole object of the transaction, it could not be permissible to exclude this obligation. No English case ever squarely presented this problem and the matter was resolved by Parliament in 1973, when, in the Supply of Goods (Implied Terms) Act (re-enacted as s. 6 of the Unfair Contract Terms Act 1977), it provided that a seller could never exclude or limit his or her obligations under s. 12(1) and 12(2). (The whole topic of excluding and limiting clauses is considered in more detail in Chapter 9).

However, the seller is permitted to contract on the basis that he or she only undertakes to transfer whatever title he or she actually has. In other words, the seller may say 'I do not know whether I am owner or not but if I am, I will transfer ownership to you'. Of course, the seller cannot do this if he or she knows he or she is not the owner and one would normally expect that the buyer would demand a significant reduction in price for taking this risk.

6-08 This possibility is governed by s. 12(3)-(5) which provides:

'12 (3) This sub-section applies to a contract of sale in the case of which there appears from the contract or is to be inferred from its circumstances an intention that the seller should transfer only such title as he or a third person may have.

(4)   In a contract to which sub-section (3) above applies there is an implied warranty that all charges or encumbrances known to the seller and not known to the buyer have been disclosed to the buyer before the contract is made.

(5)   In a contract to which sub-section (3) above applies there is also an implied warranty that none of the following will disturb the buyer's quiet possession of the goods, namely -

(a) the seller;

(b) in a case where the parties to the contract intend that the seller should transfer only such title as a third person may have, that person;

(c) anyone claiming through or under the seller or that third person otherwise than under a charge or encumbrance disclosed or known to the buyer before the contract is made.'

It will be seen that s. 12(3) envisages the possibility that it may be inferred from the circumstances, that the seller is only contracting to sell whatever title he or she has. This would obviously be unusual but an example which is often given is that of a sale by sheriff after he or she has executed a judgment debt. If, for instance, the sheriff takes possession of the television set in the judgment debtor's house and sells it, he or she will usually have no idea whether it belongs to the judgment debtor or is subject to a hire-purchase or rental agreement. It will be seen that s. 12(4) and (5) contains modified versions of the obligations which are usually implied under s. 12(2).

3 THE PASSING OF PROPERTY

This section deals with the rules of English law which decide when ownership is to pass from seller to buyer. It is worth asking first why this question is important, since it is safe to say that as a rule, the buyer is much more concerned with delivery of the goods and the seller with payment of the price. There are two main reasons. The first is that as a matter of technique, English law makes some other questions turn on the answer to this question. So as a rule, the passing of risk (discussed in Chapter 7) is linked to the passing of property, as is the seller's right to sue for the price, under s. 49(1) (as opposed to maintaining an action for damages for non-payment of the price, discussed in Chapter 10). There is nothing essential about this link. Other systems of law, for instance, have developed rules about the passing of risk, which are wholly divorced from their rules about the passing of property. The principal advantage of the English system is perhaps a certain economy of effort in dealing with two questions at the same time. The disadvantage is that the separate questions which are thus linked together may in fact demand a more sophisticated range of answers than can be provided by a single concept.

6-09

The second reason is that who owns the goods usually becomes important, if either buyer or seller becomes insolvent. Sellers, for instance, often offer credit to their customers; that is, they deliver the goods before they have been paid for. Inevitably, some buyers, having received the goods, are unable to pay for them because they have become insolvent. If the buyer has not only received possession of the goods, but also becomes the owner of them, the seller's only remedy will be to prove in the liquidation and usually this will mean that he or she will not be paid in full and, indeed, often not at all. On the other hand, if the seller still owns the goods, he or she will usually be entitled to recover possession of them, which will be a much more satisfactory remedy. This desire to improve the position of the seller in the buyer's insolvency has become so commercially important that it has lead to widespread use of 'retention of title clauses' which are discussed more fully below.

The basic rules as to the passing of property are set out in ss. 16 and 17 of the Sale of Goods Act which provide:

'16   Where there is a contract for the sale of unascertained goods no property in the goods is transferred to the buyer unless and until the goods are ascertained.

17 (1)   Where there is a contract for the sale of specific or ascertained goods the property in them is transferred to the buyer at such time as the parties to the contract intend it to be transferred.

(2)   For the purpose of ascertaining the intention of the parties regard shall be had to the terms of the contract, the conduct of the parties and the circumstances of the case.'

6-10   So the first rule is that property cannot pass if the goods are unascertained. This makes the distinction between specific and unascertained goods which was explained in Chapter 3 fundamental, since the second rule is that if the goods are specific or ascertained, the parties are free to make whatever agreement they like about when property is to pass. This second rule was adopted by English law in relation to sale of goods at a very early stage and is in marked distinction both to sale of *land*, where a formal act of conveyance is needed for an effective transfer of ownership and to *gifts* of goods, where an effective physical delivery is necessary to such a transfer. This means that where the goods are specific or ascertained, transfer of property under a sale is completely separate from questions of delivery or payment.

It is a typical feature of English contract law to make results depend on the intentions of parties. This is sometimes criticised on the ground that the parties may well have formed no relevant intention. Like many such criticisms, this is true only in part. The advantage of a rule based on intention is that it provides great flexibility to parties who know what they are doing. Where, as will often be the case, a contract is subject to standard conditions of sale or purchase, one would certainly expect to find a provision expressly dealing with the passing of property. In other cases the transaction will be set against a commercial background, which provides determinative clues to the parties' intentions. So in international sales, the parties will often provide that payment is to be 'cash against documents' and this will usually mean that property is to pass when the buyer takes up the documents and pays against them.

6-11   Nevertheless, it is undoubtedly true that there will be many cases, particularly perhaps consumer transactions, where the parties do not direct their thoughts to this question. Assistance is then provided by s. 18 which provides rules for ascertaining the intention of the parties 'unless a different intention appears'. Rules 1, 2 and 3 deal with sales of specific goods.

'18   Unless a different intention appears, the following are rules for ascertaining the intention of the parties as to the time at which the property in the goods is to pass to the buyer.

Rule 1. - Where there is an unconditional contract for the sale of specific goods in a deliverable state the property in the goods passes to the buyer when the contract is made, and it is immaterial whether the time of payment or the time of delivery, or both, be postponed.

Rule 2. - Where there is a contract for the sale of specific goods and the seller is bound to do something to the goods for the purpose of putting them into a deliverable state, the property does not pass until the thing is done and the buyer has notice that it has been done.

Rule 3. - Where there is a contract for the sale of specific goods, in a deliverable state but the seller is bound to weigh, measure, test, or do some other act or thing with reference to the goods for the purpose of ascertaining the price, the property does not pass until the act or thing is done and the buyer has notice that it has been done.'

It will be noted that rule 1 contemplates that in the case of specific goods property may pass at the moment the contract is made. However, this will not in practice be that common, since in *R. V. Ward v. Bignall* (1967)[7] it was said that in modern conditions it would not require much material to support the inference that property was to pass at a later stage. So if I select an article in a shop and hand it to the cashier, there would be a contract as soon as the cashier had signified acceptance of my offer, but a court might well hold that the property did not pass until I had paid.

Rule 1 only applies where the contract is 'unconditional' and the goods in a 'deliverable state'. In contract and sales law, the word condition bears many different meanings. In the present context it is usually taken to mean that the contract does not contain any term which suspends the passing of property until some later event. The words 'deliverable state' are defined by s. 61(5) which provides that 'Goods are in a deliverable state within the meaning of this Act when they are in such a state that the buyer would under the contract be bound to take delivery of them'.

This definition is potentially very wide, since there are many possible   **6-12** defects in the goods which would entitle the buyer to refuse to accept delivery. (This is discussed more fully in Chapters 8 and 10.) It would seem that if the goods are actually delivered to the buyer, rule 1 would not prevent property passing. So if A sells a car to B and delivers a car containing a latent defect which would have justified rejection if B had known of it, it seems that property probably passes to B on delivery. It is probable that in formulating rule 1, the draughtsman had principally in mind the situation covered by rule 2, where the goods are not defective,

---

7   [1967] 1 Q.B. 534.

but need something doing to them before the buyer is required to accept delivery. An example would be when there is a sale of a ton of coffee beans and the seller agrees to bag the beans before delivery.

Rule 4 deals with *sale or return* and provides:

'18. Rule 4 - When goods are delivered to the buyer on approval or on sale or return or other similar terms the property in goods passes to the buyer:-

> (a) when he signifies his approval or acceptance to the seller or does any other act adopting the transaction;
>
> (b) if he does not signify his approval or acceptance to the seller but retains the goods without giving notice of rejection, then, if a time has been fixed for the return of the goods, on the expiration of that time, and, if no time has been fixed, on the expiration of a reasonable time.'

The principal difficulty here is to determine exactly what is meant by 'sale or return'. There are many transactions in which there is an excellent chance in practice that the seller, if asked, will accept a return of goods and give a cash refund. Many retail shops will do this and equally publishers usually accept returns from retail booksellers. Such transactions are usually not contracts of sale or return in the strict sense, since the buyer does not have a contractual option to accept or reject the goods, but simply a commercial expectation that he or she will be able to return the goods if he or she wishes to do so.

6-13   If the transaction is one of sale or return, the buyer loses the right to return the goods if he or she approves or accepts them or otherwise adopts the transaction. This means that if the buyer does something which an honest person would not do unless he or she intended to adopt, he or she will be treated as having adopted. So in *Kirkham v. Attenborough* (1897)[8] the buyer borrowed money from a pawnbroker on the security of the goods and this was treated as an adoption. Alternatively, property may pass to the buyer under rule 4(b) because he has failed to reject in time.

Rule 5 deals with unascertained goods and provides:

'18.   Rule 5. - (1) Where there is a contract for the sale of unascertained or future goods by description, and goods of that description and in a deliverable state are unconditionally appropriated to the contract, either by the seller with the assent of the buyer or by the buyer with the assent of the seller, the property in the goods then passes to the buyer; and the assent may be express or implied, and may be given either before or after the appropriation is made.

---

8   [1897] 1 Q.B. 201.

(2)   Where, in pursuance of the contract, the seller delivers the goods to the buyer or to a carrier or other bailee or custodier (whether named by the buyer or not) for the purpose of transmission to the buyer, and does not reserve the right of disposal, he is to be taken to have unconditionally appropriated the goods to the contract.'

In practice this is the most important of the rules. We have already seen that in the sale of unascertained goods, property cannot pass until the goods are ascertained even if the parties were to try to agree otherwise. This basic principle was recently reaffirmed by the Privy Council in *Re Goldcorp Exchange Ltd* (1994)[9]. In this case, a New Zealand company dealt in gold and sold to customers on the basis that the company would store and insure the gold free of charge. They issued certificates to the customers. No specific gold was set aside for any specific customer though there were assurances (which were not kept) that a sufficient supply of gold would be held at all times to meet orders for delivery by customers. In fact, the company became hopelessly insolvent and had inadequate supplies of gold. The Privy Council held that it was elementary that property had not passed from the sellers to the buyers. This case can be usefully contrasted with *Re Stapylton Fletcher Ltd* (1995)[10]. In this case, wine merchants bought and sold wine and also sold it on the basis that they would store it for customers until it was fit to drink. In this case, the wine merchant kept the boxes of wine which they were holding for customers in a separate unit. This unit contained nothing but wine which was being stored for customers and, at all times, the right quantities of vintages were in stock and the total was in strict compliance with the customers' storage records. On the other hand, the wine merchant did not mark individual cases of wine with the customer's name, since, where as was usually the case, there was more than one case of a particular vintage, it was convenient to supply customers off the top of the pile which necessarily meant that individual cases were not allocated. The wine merchants became insolvent. In this case, it was held that the wine was sufficiently ascertained for the customers to become tenants in common of the stock in the proportion that their goods bore to the total in store for the time being. This decision is very important because it shows that the ascertainment rule does not prevent two or more owning goods in common where there is an undivided bulk. Once the goods are ascertained the property will pass at the time agreed by the parties. Where the parties have reached no express agreement rule 5 propounds a test based on appropriation.

---

[9]   [1994] 2 All E.R. 806.
[10] [1995] 1 All E.R. 192.

6-14   In some cases ascertainment and appropriation may take place at the same time. This was so in *Karlhamns Oljefabriker v. Eastport Navigation* (1982)[11] (discussed in Chapter 3). This is quite likely to be the case where the goods are appropriated by delivery to a carrier as happens particularly in international sales (though in such sales there are often express agreements as to the passing of property). So if the seller contracts to sell 1,000 tons Western White Wheat cif Avonmouth and puts 1,000 tons of Western White Wheat aboard a ship bound for Avonmouth this may both ascertain and appropriate the goods. In many such cases however the seller will load 2,000 tons having sold 1,000 tons to A, and 1,000 tons to B. In such a case the goods will not be ascertained until the first 1,000 tons are unloaded at the destination. If the Sale of Goods Bill 1995 becomes law this rule will be altered so that A and P may become tenants in common of the whole 2,000 tons, even before the goods become ascertained. Even where the seller puts only 1,000 tons on board this will not necessarily constitute appropriation because he may not at that stage have committed himself to using *that* 1,000 tons to perform *that* contract.

This example brings out the special meaning of appropriation in this context. Suppose a wine merchant has 100 cases of Meursault 1985 in his cellars and advertises it to his customers at £15 per bottle or £175 per case. Not surprisingly he quickly receives orders for the 100 cases and as a first step labels each of the cases with the name of the customer for whom it is intended. In a sense he has clearly appropriated the cases to the contracts but not for the purposes of rule 5. This was clearly decided in *Carlos Federspiel v. Twigg* (1957)[12] where the seller had agreed to sell a number of bicycles to the buyer. The seller had packed the bicycles, marked them with the buyer's name and told the buyer the shipping marks. The seller then went insolvent. The buyer argued that the bicycles had been appropriated to its contract and that property had passed to it. This argument was rejected on the grounds that the seller could properly have had a change of mind and appropriated new bicycles to the contract.

It is essential that there is a degree of irrevocability in the appropriation. It is this which makes delivery to the carrier often the effective act of appropriation.

---

11 [1982] 1 All E.R. 208.
12 [1957] 1 Lloyds Rep. 240.

4 RETENTION OF TITLE CLAUSES[13]

We have seen in the previous section that, subject to the goods being **6-15** ascertained, the parties may make whatever agreement they like about when property is to pass. So property may pass even though the goods have not been delivered and the price not yet paid. Conversely, the parties may agree that the property is not to pass even though the goods have been delivered and paid for. It is very likely that a seller who employs standard conditions of sale and normally gives his or her customers credit will wish to provide that property does not pass simply on delivery but only at some later stage such as when payment is made. This possibility is clearly implicit in ss. 17 and 18. It is, however, explicitly stated in s. 19.

'19. (1) Where there is a contract for the sale of specific goods or where goods are subsequently appropriated to the contract, the seller may, by the terms of the contract or appropriation, reserve the right of disposal of the goods until certain conditions are fulfilled; and in such a case, notwithstanding the delivery of the goods to the buyer, or to a carrier or other bailee or custodier for the purpose of transmission to the buyer, the property in the goods does not pass to the buyer until the conditions imposed by the seller are fulfilled.

(2)   Where goods are shipped, and by the bill of lading the goods are deliverable to the order of the seller or his agent, the seller is *prima facie* to be taken to reserve the right of disposal.

(3)   Where the seller of goods draws on the buyer for the price, and transmits the bill of exchange and bill of lading to the buyer together to secure acceptance or payment of the bill of exchange, the buyer is bound to return the bill of lading if he does not honour the bill of exchange, and if he wrongfully retains the bill of lading the property in the goods does not pass to him.'

It will be seen that s. 19 talks about the seller reserving 'the right of **6-16** disposal of the goods'. This, despite appearances, is effectively another synonym for ownership. The expression has been of long standing use in relation to export sales and bills of lading and it is worth spending a moment explaining the operation of the bill of lading as it gives an excellent example of the reservation of the right of disposal. Before the invention of the aeroplane all export sales in this country involved the

---

13   This topic appears to have produced more books than the rest of sales law put together. See Davies, *Effective Retention of Title*; McCormack, *Reservation of Title* and Parris, *Effective Retention of Title Clauses*. Wheeler *Reservation of Title Clauses* is not an exposition of the law but rather an examination of how effective such clauses are to protect sellers in practice. See also Palmer 5 J *Contract Law* 175; McCormack 12 *Legal Studies* 195.

use of sea carriage and this is still the predominant way of moving goods. Most sellers do not have ships of their own and therefore performance of the contract of sale will normally involve entrusting the goods to a sea carrier. In the classical arrangement the seller would put the goods on board a ship having made arrangements for them to be carried to a seaport in the buyer's country. The seller would usually receive from the sea carrier a bill of lading. The bill of lading fulfils three distinct functions. It acts as a receipt so as to show the goods have been loaded on board the ship; it acts as evidence of the contract between the seller and the sea carrier for the carriage of the goods to their destination and it operates as a 'document of title'. It is this third role which concerns us here. Since the 18th century it has been recognised that someone who has put goods on board a ship and received a bill of lading has control of the goods in a way which enables him or her to transfer that control to another person by a transfer of the bill of lading. This is because by mercantile custom the captain of the ship would deliver the cargo to the holder of the bill of lading provided it had been suitably endorsed. This meant, for instance, that the seller could put goods on board the ship not yet having sold them and while they were on the high seas dispose of them. Buyers would often pay for the goods against the bill of lading and other documents knowing that when the ship arrived they would be able to get the cargo from the master. So the bill of lading provided a means of disposal of the goods. The seller could have sold the goods and property could have passed to the buyer without any dealings with the bill of lading. The buyer would then, however, have had difficulty in getting the goods off the ship. In practice a buyer who knows that the goods are on board the ship is very unlikely to want to pay in cash unless he or she receives the bill of lading or some other equivalent document. In some commodity trades there may be several sales and sub-sales of the goods while they are on the high seas, each effected by transferring the bill of lading against payment. Section 19(1) expressly recognises this general possibility and s. 19(2) expressly recognises the specific possibility that the seller will take the bill of lading to his or her own order and that this will normally show that he or she is reserving the right of disposal[14]. Because commercial custom recognises the effectiveness of transfers of bills of lading made in the proper form, the seller can dispose of the bill of lading and the goods by endorsing it to the buyer (that is by writing across the face of the bill of lading an instruction to deliver to the buyer).

6-17   In the context of export/import sales this has long been well recognised as standard practice. It has also, no doubt, long been

---

[14] Even where the buyer has paid 80% of the price before shipment. *Mitsui & Co. v. Flota Mercante Grancolombiana* [1988] 1 W.L.R. 1145.

standard practice for sellers supplying goods on credit in domestic sales to have simple clauses saying that the goods are theirs until they are paid. No problem arises with such clauses. This should always have been clear but some deviant decisions in Scotland required it to be reaffirmed. In *Armour v. Thyssen Edelstahlwerke A.G.* (1990)[15] where the House of Lords overturned decisions of the Scottish courts treating a simple reservation of title as creating a charge. Lord Keith of Kinkel, delivering the principal speech, said:

> 'I am, however, unable to regard a provision reserving title to the seller until payment of all debts due to him by the buyer as amounting to the creation by the buyer of a right to security in favour of the seller. Such a provision does in a sense give the seller security for the unpaid debts of the buyer. But it does so by way of a legitimate retention of title, not by virtue of any right over his own property conferred by the buyer.'

However, in the last 20 years much more elaborate and complex clauses have begun regularly to be used. The starting point of modern discussion is the decision of the Court of Appeal in *Aluminium Industrie v. Romalpa* (1976)[16]. This case has been so influential that the sort of complex clauses which are used are quite often referred to as Romalpa clauses (or alternatively as retention or reservation of title clauses). In the *Romalpa* case the plaintiff was a Dutch company which sold aluminium foil to the defendant, an English company. The plaintiff had elaborate standard conditions of sale which provided, among other things:

(a) that ownership of the foil was to be transferred only when the buyer had met all that was owing to the seller;

(b) required the buyer to store the foil in such a way that it was clearly the property of the seller until it had been paid for;

(c) that articles manufactured from the foil were to become the property of the seller as security for payment and that until such payment had been made the buyer was to keep the articles manufactured as 'fiduciary owner' for the seller and if required to store them separately so that they could be recognised.

The buyer was permitted to sell finished products to third parties on condition that, if requested, he or she would hand over to the seller any claims which he or she might have against said buyers.

It is important to note the width of the basic clause about transfer of ownership. The goods were being supplied regularly on credit terms. In **6-18**

---

15   [1990] 3 All E.R. 481; [1991] 2 A.C. 339.
16   [1976] 2 All E.R. 552; [1976] 1 W.L.R. 676.

such a situation it is perfectly possible even though the goods are being punctiliously paid for on time that there is always money outstanding to the seller so that property never passes at all. So if the standard credit terms of the trade are to pay 28 days after delivery of the invoice and there are deliveries of goods every 21 days there will nearly always be money owing to the seller, even though the buyer is paying on time. In the *Romalpa* case itself the buyer eventually became insolvent owing the plaintiff over £120,000. The buyer had some £50,000 worth of foil and also had, in a separate bank account, some £35,000 which represented the proceeds of foil which the plaintiff had supplied to the defendant and which the defendant had then sub-sold. The Court of Appeal held that the plaintiff was entitled both to recover the foil and also the £35,000 which was in the separate account.

This case illustrates in a dramatic way the practical importance of these retention of title clauses. They are basically a device to protect the seller against the buyer's insolvency. If the buyer remains solvent the retention of title clause does little more than involve it in some tiresome extra paperwork. This is because although the buyer may in theory be holding substantial quantities of goods which belong to the seller, it will not, so long as it is solvent, be liable to redeliver the goods to the seller, unless it commits some major breach of contract which entitles the seller to bring the contract to an end. However, if the buyer becomes insolvent, a seller who has a valid retention of title clause will have a significantly improved position. Small businesses become insolvent every day and large businesses not infrequently. What usually happens in such cases is that nearly all of the assets fall into the hands of the Inland Revenue and the Customs and Excise who have preferential claims and into the hands of the bank who will have taken a mortgage over the company's premises and a floating charge over the company's other assets. Arguably the English insolvency law regime favours the tax authorities and the banks too much at the expense of ordinary trade creditors. Retention of title clauses can be seen as an attempt to redress the balance.

Such a step is perfectly effective if all that is done is to use the power of s. 19 to delay the passing of ownership from seller to buyer.

6-19   However, many sellers, like the one in the *Romalpa* case, have much more elaborate clauses. Since 1976 these clauses have been the subject of a number of litigated cases and in many of them the courts have held that the clause is ineffective. This is partly because these decisions have turned on the particular wording of specific clauses and partly on a perception by the judges that the sellers, in seeking to do too much, have overreached themselves. The general problem which lies behind the cases is that, whatever the abstract legal analysis, the seller's practical objective is to create a form of security interest in the goods. The companies legislation provides a limited number of possibilities for the creation of security interests in the property of companies (in practice the buyer has always been a company in the litigated cases. If the buyer were not a company, these difficulties would disappear). In particular, in a number of cases the other creditors of the buyer have successfully argued that the retention of title clause is invalid because it amounts to an unregistered charge over the company's assets. This argument does not succeed if all that the seller has done is to have a straightforward s. 19 clause providing that ownership remains with it until it has been paid (*Clough Mill v. Martin* (1984)[17]). This is permissible even if the seller retains ownership over goods which have been paid for, because such ownership would be subject to an implied term that the seller could only deal with the goods to the extent needed to discharge the balance of the outstanding debts.

So, retention of title clauses work perfectly satisfactorily if the buyer intends to keep the goods in its hands unaltered. However, buyers often intend either to resell the goods or to incorporate the goods in a larger product, or to use the goods as raw materials for the manufacture of goods. In an attempt to secure rights in cases of this kind sellers have often adopted elaborate clauses of the kind mentioned in the discussion above of the *Romalpa* case. It is necessary, therefore, to say something about these more complex clauses.

In some cases the contract has provided that the buyer is to have legal **6-20** ownership of the goods but that 'equitable and beneficial' ownership is to remain in the seller. Such a clause was considered in *Re Bond Worth* (1979)[18] where the goods supplied were raw materials used by the buyer for the manufacture of carpets. Slade J held that the clause was invalid as being an attempt to create an unregistered charge. It seems, therefore, that in general the seller must attempt to retain legal ownership. However, this will not work where the goods are being incorporated into larger goods unless the goods remain identifiable. An interesting case in this respect is *Hendy Lennox v. Grahame Puttick Ltd.* (1984)[19] where the goods were diesel engines which were being used by the buyer for incorporation into diesel generating sets. The engines remained readily identifiable because all the engines were those provided by the seller and each engine had a serial number. Furthermore, the engines could, with relative ease, have been disconnected and removed from the generating sets. It was held that in such a situation the seller could continue to assert rights of ownership even after the engines had been incorporated into the generators.

---

[17] [1984] 3 All E.R. 982; [1985] 1 W.L.R. 111.
[18] [1979] 3 All E.R. 919; [1980] Ch. 228.
[19] [1984] 2 All E.R. 152; [1984] 1 W.L.R. 485.

In other cases, the goods are incorporated into finished products in a way in which it would be impossible to unscramble the omelette and separate out the constituent eggs. Sellers have sometimes sought to provide in this situation that they retain ownership in the raw materials or that the finished product is to be treated as theirs. This would probably present no problems if the seller had supplied all the ingredients for the finished products but in practice this has never been the facts of a reported case. One might envisage a case in which the finished product is made up partly of goods supplied by seller A and partly of goods supplied by seller B, each of whom has provided that the finished product is to belong to him. This case too has never been reported. The cases which have arisen have been those in which one of the ingredients in the finished product has been provided by a seller who employed a retention of title clause and the other ingredients by sellers who did not. In practice, in all of these cases the courts have held that the seller does not in fact retain a valid interest in the finished product. So in *Borden v. Scottish Timber Products* (1981)[20] a seller who supplied resin to a buyer who used it to manufacturer chipboard obtained no property interest in the chipboard and in *Re Peachdart* (1984)[21] a seller who supplied leather for the making of handbags failed successfully to assert a claim against the handbags. It is not clear whether the seller could improve on these cases by more sophisticated drafting. Suppose a seller on the facts of *Re Peachdart* had provided in the contract that the handbags were to be the joint property of the seller and the manufacturer. It is at least possible that this would create rights which the court would protect[22]. In New Zealand it has been held that a seller of trees could retain ownership rights after the trees have been converted into logs by the buyer[23].

6-21   The buyer may have bought the goods intending to resell them. Normally the retention of title clause will not be effective to prevent the sub-buyer acquiring a good title for reasons which will become clearer after the reading of the next section (see *Four Point Garage v. Carter* (1985)[24]). However, a seller may insert a clause in the contract providing that the buyer is to have permission to sub-sell the goods but that the proceeds of such sub-sale are to be put into a separate bank account

[20] [1981] Ch. 25.
[21] [1984] Ch. 131.
[22] See *Coleman v. Harvey* [1989] 1 N.Z.L.R. 723; *Hudson* [1991] L.M.C.L.Q. 23.
[23] *New Zealand Forest Products v. Pongakawa Sawmill* [1991] 3 N.Z.L.R. 112.
[24] [1985] 3 All E.R. 12.

which is to be held on trust for the seller. If the buyer in fact opens such an account and pays the proceeds into it this would be an effective clause. In practice a buyer who is having financial problems and is approaching insolvency is very likely to find ways of paying the proceeds of sub-sales into an account with which he or she can deal so that such a clause will not provide complete practical protection for the seller.

5 TRANSFER OF TITLE WHERE THE SELLER IS NOT THE OWNER

In this section we consider cases where the seller was not in fact the owner nor the authorised agent of the owner at the time of the sale. This situation may arise in a range of cases running from the situation where the seller has stolen the goods all the way to a case where the seller honestly believes that he is the owner of the goods but has himself been misled by a previous seller. In this type of case there is a conflict of interest between that of the original owner of the goods who is seeking to recover them or their value, and the ultimate buyer who has paid good money for goods which he believed the seller to be entitled to sell to him. In general, it is desirable to protect the interests both of the owners of property and of honest buyers who pay a fair price. In the case of transactions in land the choice comes down unhesitatingly in favour of protecting the interests of owners. This is possible because transferring ownership of land is a highly formal act normally carried out by lawyers. In practice, therefore, it is extremely difficult for an honest buyer who employs a competent lawyer not to discover that the seller is not entitled to sell. In practice it would be extremely difficult to apply this technique to transactions in goods. Some legal systems have therefore decided that the primary interest is to protect the honest buyer who pays a fair price and has no ground for suspecting that his seller is not the owner. English law has not taken this choice, however. Instead it has started from the position that the seller cannot normally transfer any better rights than he himself has. This is often put in the form of the Latin maxim *nemo dat quod non habet* (roughly, no one can transfer what he does not have). Lawyers often talk in shorthand about the *nemo dat* rule. However, although it is clear that this is the basic rule, it is equally clear that it is subject to a substantial number of exceptions. Most of the exceptions are set out in ss. 21-26 of the Sale of Goods Act 1979 and we will discuss each exception in turn.

6-22

Estoppel

6-23   Section 21(1) of the Act provides:

'Subject to this Act, where goods are sold by a person who is not their owner, and who does not sell them under the authority or with the consent of the owner, the buyer acquires no better title to the goods than the seller had, unless the owner of the goods is by his conduct precluded from denying the seller's authority to sell.'

For present purposes the sting of this section lies in its tail which is an application of the general legal doctrine of estoppel. The operation of the doctrine is to prevent (estop) a party from advancing an argument which he or she would otherwise be entitled to put forward. So, for instance, a party may be prevented from putting forward an argument because it has been the subject matter of a previous judicial decision on the same facts which is binding on him or her. An example of the operation of doctrine in the present context is *Eastern Distributors Ltd. v. Goldring* (1957)[25]. In this case the owner of a van wished to raise money on it and for this purpose entered into an arrangement with a car dealer which involved the deception of a finance company. The scheme was that the dealer would pretend to have bought the van and to be letting it to the owner on hire-purchase terms. The owner signed in blank one of the finance company's hire-purchase agreements, together with a delivery note stating that he had taken delivery of the van. The dealer then completed a further form purporting to offer to sell the van to the finance company. The result was that the finance company paid the dealer. On these facts it could perhaps have been argued that the owner had actually authorised the dealer to sell his van to the finance company. However, the case was decided on the basis that the owner had not authorised the dealer to sell the van to the finance company but that he was estopped from so arguing. This was on the basis that by signing the forms in the way he had, he had made it easy for the dealer to deceive the finance company as to who was the true owner of the van.

6-24   It is common in analysing the operation of estoppel in this area to distinguish between estoppel by representation, which arises where it could be said that the true owner has represented that someone else has authority to sell the goods, and estoppel by negligence which arises where the true owner has behaved carelessly in respect of the goods in such a way as to enable the goods to be dealt with in a way which causes loss to a third party. However, in practice, the courts have been very cautious in applying either limb of the doctrine. In particular, it is clear that it does not by the mere act of the owner putting his or her goods

---

[25]   [1957] 2 Q.B. 600.

into the hands of someone else, represent that that person has authority to sell them, nor is it negligent to do so unless it is possible to analyse the transaction in such a way as to support the argument that the true owner owed a duty of care in respect of the goods to the party who has been deceived.

The narrow scope of both estoppel by representation and estoppel by negligence is shown by *Moorgate Mercantile v. Twitchings* (1977)[26] in which the majority of the House of Lords rejected the application of both doctrines. This case concerned a car which had been let on hire-purchase terms. It is so common for parties, who have taken cars on hire-purchase, to sell them for cash before they have completed the hire-purchase contract that the hire-purchase companies set up an organisation called Hire-Purchase Information (H.P.I.) which acts as a central registry of hire-purchase transactions in relation to motor cars. Membership of the organisation is not compulsory but most finance companies belong to it and many car dealers are affiliated to it so that they are able to obtain information. The normal practice is for finance companies which are members to notify all credit transactions involving cars. Then if the car is offered to another dealer or finance company they can check with H.P.I. as to whether there is an existing credit agreement in relation to the car. This system obviously makes it much more difficult for a car subject to a credit agreement to be disposed of without the agreement being revealed. (Obviously it does not prevent direct sale to another member of public.) In the present case, the plaintiff finance company let a car on hire-purchase to A. The plaintiff was a member of H.P.I. and normally registered all its agreements with it. For some reason, which was never explained, the particular transaction with A was not registered and a few months later he offered the car for sale to the defendant. A told the defendant he was the owner of the car and when the defendant contacted H.P.I. he was told that the car was not registered with them. The defendant bought the car from A and in due course sold it to B. Later the plaintiff discovered that the car had been sold and brought an action against the defendant. The defendant argued that there was estoppel both by representation and by negligence. These arguments, though successful in the Court of Appeal, were rejected by a majority of three to two in the House of Lords. The majority view was that there was no estoppel by representation since no representation had been made by the plaintiff; any representation which had been made had been made by H.P.I. but it had simply said, which was true, that the car was not registered with it. H.P.I. was not in any case the agent of the plaintiff for the purpose of making any representation about the car. One

---

[26] [1977] A.C. 890.

ground for rejecting arguments based on estoppel by negligence was that it had not been proved that failure to register was the plaintiff's fault. (It was never proved how the failure had taken place). However, the majority in the House of Lords would have rejected the argument based on estoppel by negligence even if it could have been shown that the plaintiff had failed to register this particular transaction. This was on the basis that the plaintiff owed no duty of care to other finance companies or to dealers to register the transaction. In coming to this conclusion great weight was attached to the fact that the whole scheme was voluntary and not mandatory. This case brings out very clearly the policy issues involved and the cautious way in which the courts have in practice decided to apply the doctrine of estoppel.

6-25   Another restriction of the scope of s. 21(1) was revealed by the decision in *Shaw v. Commissioner of Police* (1987)[27]. In this case the claimant, Mr Natalegawa, a student from Indonesia, owned a red Porsche. He advertised it for sale in a newspaper and received a call from a gentleman calling himself Jonathan London who said he was a car dealer and was interested in buying the car on behalf of a client. The claimant allowed London to take delivery of the car and gave him a letter saying that he had sold the car to London and disclaiming further legal responsibility for it. In return he received a cheque for £17,250 which in due course proved worthless. London agreed to sell the car to the plaintiff for £11,500, £10,000 to be paid by banker's draft. When London presented the draft the bank refused to cash it and London disappeared. In due course, the police took possession of the car and both the plaintiff and the claimant sought possession of it. The Court of Appeal held that as far as s. 21 was concerned the case would have fallen within its scope if the sale by London to the plaintiff had been completed. It was clear, however, that as far as the contract between the plaintiff and London was concerned, property in the car (if London had had it) was only to pass when London was paid. Since London had never been paid, the transaction was an agreement to sell and not a sale. This is logical because on the facts the plaintiff would not have become the owner of the car even if London had been an owner or an authorised agent. It would be paradoxical if the plaintiff were to be in a better position because London was a dishonest man.

Sale in market overt

6-26   Section 22(1) of the Sale of Goods Act 1979 provides:

---

[27]   [1987] 3 All E.R. 305; [1987] 1 W.L.R. 1332.

'Where goods are sold in market overt, according to the usage of the market, the buyer acquires a good title to the goods, provided he buys them in good faith and without notice of any defect or want of title on the part of the seller.'

As the language suggests this is a very old, indeed the oldest, exception to the general rule. It starts from the perception that a dishonest person is less likely to sell goods that he or she does not own in an open market than in a private sale. This rule reflects the supervision given to markets in the Middle Ages and may well have been historically true. This rationale has little place in modern business conditions and the exception has been removed by the Sale of Goods (Amendment) Act 1994.

Sale under a voidable title

Section 23 of the Sale of Goods Act 1979 provides:

'When the seller of goods has a voidable title to them, but his title has not been avoided at the time of the sale, the buyer acquires a good title to the goods, provided he buys them in good faith and without notice of the seller's defect of title.'

This exception is much more important in practice. It applies where the seller, instead of having no title at all, has a title which is liable to be avoided. The most obvious example would be where the seller had obtained possession of the goods by fraud. Where a contract is induced by one party's fraud the result is not that the contract is void but that it is voidable, that is liable to be set aside by the deceived party. Where an owner of goods has parted with them to a fraudulent buyer, he or she is entitled to set aside the contract and, if he or she acts in time, can recover the goods. However, if the fraudulent person has meanwhile sold the goods on to an innocent buyer, that innocent buyer will obtain a title which is better than that of the original owner. This is the point of s. 23.

A critical question, therefore, is what does the original owner have to do to set the voidable contract aside? Telling the fraudulent person or taking the goods from him or her would certainly do but in practice the fraudulent person and the goods have usually disappeared. In *Car and Universal Finance Ltd. v. Caldwell* (1965)[28] the Court of Appeal held that it was possible to avoid the contract without either telling the fraudulent person or retaking possession of the goods. In that case the owner had sold his car to a rogue and received a worthless cheque in return. The next morning the owner presented the cheque at the bank and

---

[28] [1965] 1 Q.B. 525.

discovered that it was worthless. He immediately informed the police and the motoring organisations. It was held that the sale had been effectively avoided on the grounds that it is sufficient to do all that can in practice be done to set the transaction aside. Many commentators were surprised at this decision and indeed the opposing view was taken in Scotland on virtually identical facts in *McLeod v. Kerr* (1965)[29].

In practice however, whether right or wrong, the decision in the *Caldwell* case is not as important as it appears at first sight because similar facts will usually fall within the scope of another exception discussed below (buyer in possession after sale).

Seller in possession after sale

6-28

Section 24 of the Sale of Goods Act 1979 provides:

'Where a person having sold goods continues or is in possession of the goods, or of the documents of title to the goods, the delivery or transfer by that person, or by a mercantile agent acting for him, of the goods or documents of title under any sale, pledge, or disposition thereof, to any person receiving the same in good faith and without notice of the previous sale, has the same effect as if the person making the delivery or transfer were expressly authorised by the owner of goods to make the same.'

It is easy to apply this section to the case where the seller simply sells goods to A and then, without ever having delivered them to A, sells the same goods to B.

Difficulties have arisen, however, because the section talks of the seller who continues or is in possession of the goods. Suppose that a car dealer sells a car to A who pays for it and takes it away and then the following day brings it back for some small defect to be rectified. While the car is at the dealer's premises, the dealer sells it to B. It would be possible to read the section as giving B's rights precedence over those of A but it is quite clear that if A had taken his car to any other dealer who had sold it to B, A's rights would have prevailed over those of B. It would be very odd to make the positions of A and B depend on whether A takes his car for service to the person from whom he has bought it or to someone else. In fact the courts have not read the section in this way but they have given different explanations for not doing so.

6-29

In *Staffordshire Motor Guarantee v. British Wagon* (1934)[30] a dealer sold a lorry to a finance company who then hired it back to him under a hire-

---

29 [1965] S.C. 253.
30 [1934] 2 K.B. 304.

purchase agreement. The dealer then, in breach of the hire-purchase agreement, sold the lorry to another buyer. It was held that the rights of the finance company prevailed over those of the second buyer. The explanation given was that for s. 24 to apply the seller must continue in possession 'as a seller'. However, this view was later rejected by the Privy Council on appeal from Australia in *Pacific Motor Auctions v. Motor Credits* (1965)[31] and by the Court of Appeal in *Worcester Works Finance v. Cooden Engineering* (1972)[32]. In these cases it was said that the crucial question was whether the seller's possession was physically continuous. If it was, as in the *Staffordshire Motor Guarantee* case, then s. 24 applied.

If there has been a break in possession so that the buyer has, even for a short time, had the goods in his or her hands although he or she has later re-delivered them to the seller then s. 24 does not apply. This obviously covers the case of the buyer who takes the car back to be serviced the following day, but it means that s. 24 also applies to the rather common commercial case where a motor dealer transfers ownership to a finance company or a bank but remains in possession. This is a common means of financing the stock which the dealer has on his or her floor and enables more stock to be carried than if the dealer had to carry the full cash cost of the cars. It is in effect a form of security for the lender against the dealer's stock. This form of transaction may well give the lender adequate security in the case of the insolvency of the dealer, but s. 24 will prevent it giving the lender adequate protection against the dishonest dealer who sells the cars and disappears with the proceeds.

Buyer in possession after sale

Section 25 of the Sale of Goods Act 1979 provides: 6-30

'25.(1) Where a person having bought or agreed to buy goods obtains, with the consent of the seller, possession of the goods or the documents of title to the goods, the delivery or transfer by that person, or by a mercantile agent acting for him, of the goods or documents of title, under any sale, pledge, or other disposition thereof, to any person receiving the same in good faith and without notice of any lien or other right of the original seller in respect of the goods, has the same effect as if the person making the delivery or transfer were a mercantile agent in possession of the goods or documents of title with the consent of the owner.

(2) For the purposes of subsection (1) above -

---

[31] [1965] A.C. 867.
[32] [1972] 1 Q.B. 210.

(a) the buyer under a conditional sale agreement is to be taken not to be a person who has bought or agreed to buy goods, and

(b) 'conditional sale agreement' means an agreement for the sale of goods which is a consumer credit agreement within the meaning of the Consumer Credit Act 1974 under which the purchase price or any part of it is payable by instalments, and the property in the goods is to remain in the seller (notwithstanding that the buyer is to be in possession of the goods) until such conditions as to the payment of instalments or otherwise as may be specified in the agreement are fulfilled.'

It will be seen that this section is in a sense the reverse of s. 24 since it deals with the situation where possession of the goods has passed to the buyer before ownership has passed to him or her and permits such a buyer to transfer ownership to a sub-buyer. The wording talks of 'a person having bought or agreed to buy goods'. Normally, if the buyer has bought the goods there would be a complete contract of sale and property would have passed to him or her. In that case of course, he or she would be in a position to transfer ownership to a sub-buyer without any question of s. 25 arising. The section is concerned with the situation where the buyer has obtained possession of the goods (or the documents of title to the goods) with the consent of the seller but without becoming owner.

6-31   The section does not apply where someone has obtained goods without having agreed to buy them. So in *Shaw v. Commissioner of Police* (1987)[33] a car had been obtained from the owner on the basis that the person obtaining it might have a client who might be willing to buy it. It was held that he was not a buyer within the meaning of s. 25 and was not therefore in a position to transfer ownership to a sub-buyer. In the same way, a customer under a hire-purchase agreement is not a buyer for the purpose of s. 25 because in such a case the customer has only agreed to hire the goods and is given an option to buy the goods which he or she is not legally obliged to exercise even though commercially it is extremely likely that he or she will (see discussion in Chapter 2). On the other hand, a customer who has agreed to buy the goods but has been given credit is a buyer within s. 25, even though the agreement provides that he or she is not to become the owner until he or she has paid for the goods. Section 25(2) contains a statutory modification of this rule in the case where the buyer has taken under a 'conditional sale agreement' as defined in s. 25(2)(b), that is where the price is to be paid by instalments and falls within the scope of the Consumer Credit Act 1974. The reason

---

33   [1987] 3 All ER E.R. 305

for this exception is to make the law about conditional sale agreements within the Consumer Credit Act the same as for hire-purchase agreements within the Consumer Credit Act.

Section 25 has important effects on the reasoning contained in *Car and Universal Finance v. Caldwell* (1965)[34] discussed above. In some cases of this kind, although the buyer's voidable title would have been avoided he or she would still be a buyer in possession within s. 25. This was shown in *Newtons of Wembley Ltd. v. Williams* (1965)[35] where the plaintiff agreed to sell a car to A on the basis that the property was not to pass until the whole purchase price had been paid or a cheque had been honoured. A issued a cheque and was given possession of the car but in due course his cheque bounced. The plaintiff took immediate steps to avoid the contract as in the *Caldwell* case and after he had done this A sold the car to B in a London street market and B sold the car to the defendant. The Court of Appeal held that although the plaintiff had avoided A's title, A was still a buyer in possession of the car and that B had therefore obtained a good title from A when he bought from him in good faith and had taken possession of the car. It was an important part of the Court of Appeal's reasoning that the sale by A to B had taken place in the ordinary course of business of a mercantile agent (see 6-32).

Agents and mercantile agents

In practice most sales are made by agents since most sellers are companies and employ agents to carry on their business. This presents no problem where, as would usually be the case, agents make contracts which they are authorised to make. Furthermore, under general contract law, agents bind the principal not only when they do things which they are actually authorised to do, but also when they do things which they appear to be authorised to do. The common law concerning principal and agent is expressly preserved in the Sale of Goods Act by s. 62.

6-32

However, it is clear that in the law of sale things have been developed by use of a concept of 'mercantile agents' which is wider than that of agency in the general law of contract and this development arose because of a limitation which was imposed on the general law of agency. If I put my car into the hands of a motor dealer to sell on my behalf, I will normally be bound by the contract which he or she makes even though he or she goes outside my authority, for instance by accepting a lower price than I have agreed[36]. However, if instead of selling the car,

34 [1965] 1 Q.B. 525.
35 [1965] 1 Q.B. 560.
36 *Lloyds and Scottish Finance Ltd. v. Williamson* [1965] 1 All E.R. 641; [1965] 1 W.L.R. 404.

the dealer pledges it as security for a loan, he or she would not be treated as having apparent authority to do so. This is so, even though from the point of view of someone dealing with the dealer his or her relationship to the car looks quite the same whether he or she is selling it or pledging it.

The pledging of goods and documents of title is a very important part of financing commercial transactions in some trades. So people importing large amounts of commodities, such as grain or coffee, may very likely pledge the goods or documents of title to the goods, in order to borrow money against them. It was felt unsatisfactory therefore to have this distinction between the agent who sells and the agent who pledges and this was the subject of statutory amendment by a series of Factors Acts starting in 1823 and culminating in the Factors Act 1889.

6-33 The Factors Act 1889 continues in force after the passage of the Sale of Goods Act 1893 and 1979. Section 21(2) of the Sale of Goods Act provides that:

'... nothing in this Act affects -

(a) the provisions of the Factors Acts or any enactment enabling the apparent owner of goods to dispose of them as if he were their true owner.'

Sections 8 and 9 of the Factors Act provide:

'8 Where a person, having sold goods, continues, or is, in possession of the goods or of the documents of title to the goods, the delivery or transfer by that person, or by a mercantile agent acting for him, of the goods or documents of title under any sale, pledge, or other disposition thereof, *or under any agreement for sale, pledge, or other disposition thereof,* to any person receiving the same in good faith and without notice of the previous sale, shall have the same effect as if the person making the delivery or transfer were expressly authorised by the owner of the goods to make the same.

9 Where a person, having bought or agreed to buy goods, obtains with the consent of the seller possession of the goods or the documents of title to the goods, the delivery or transfer, by that person or by a mercantile agent acting for him, of the goods or documents of title, under any sale, pledge, or other disposition thereof, *or under any agreement for sale, pledge, or other disposition thereof,* to any person receiving the same in good faith and without notice of any lien or other right of the original seller in respect of the goods, shall have the same effect as if the person making the delivery or transfer were a mercantile agent in possession of the goods or documents of title with the consent of the owner.'

It would be seen that these provisions are very similar to the provisions of ss. 24 and 25 of the Sale of Goods Act. The difference is the presence of the words in italics in the text above. A key question is clearly what is meant by a 'mercantile agent'. This is defined by s. 1(1) of the Factors Act as meaning 'a mercantile agent having in the customary course of his business as such agent authority either to sell goods, or to consign goods for the purpose of sale, or to buy goods, or to raise money on the security of goods'. The effect of dealings by mercantile agents is set out in s. 2 of the Factors Act:

'2 (1)   Where a mercantile agent is, with the consent of the owner, in possession of goods or of the documents of title to goods, any sale, pledge, or other disposition of the goods, made by him when acting in the ordinary course of business of a mercantile agent, shall, subject to the provisions of this Act, be as valid as if he were expressly authorised by the owner of the goods to make the same; provided that the person taking under the disposition acts in good faith, and has not at the time of the disposition notice that the person making the disposition has not authority to make the same.

(2)   Where a mercantile agent has, with the consent of the owner, been in possession of goods or of the documents of title to goods, any sale, pledge, or other disposition, which would have been valid if the consent had continued, shall be valid notwithstanding the determination of the consent: provided that the person taking under the disposition has not at the time thereof notice that the consent has been determined.

(3)   Where a mercantile agent has obtained possession of any documents of title to goods by reason of his being or having been, with the consent of the owner, in possession of the goods represented thereby, or of any other documents of title to the goods, his possession of the first-mentioned documents shall, for the purposes of this Act, be deemed to be with the consent of the owner.

(4)   For the purposes of this Act the consent of the owner shall be presumed in the absence of evidence to the contrary.'

The most important limitation on the width of the power given by s. 2 is that in order for the mercantile agent to be able to pass title he or she must not only be in possession with the owner's consent, but must be in possession *as a mercantile agent* with the owner's consent. So, for instance, a car dealer who has both a sale room and a service facility is clearly a mercantile agent and has the consent of his or her service customers to have possession of their cars for service, but if he or she were to put one of these cars into the sale room and sell it, this would not be a transaction protected by the Factors Acts because he or she would not have had possession of the car as a mercantile agent, but rather as a repairer.

6-34

An interesting case in this connection is *Pearson v. Rose and Young* (1951)[37] where the plaintiff delivered his car to a mercantile agent in order to obtain offers but with no authority to sell it. The agent succeeded in obtaining the log book by a trick in circumstances where it was clear that the owner had not consented to the dealer having possession of the log book. Having got both the log book and the car, the dealer then dishonestly sold it. The Court of Appeal held that this was not a transaction protected by the Factors Act. The reason was that although the dealer had possession of the car with the owner's consent, he did not have possession of the log book with the owner's consent. He could, of course, have sold the car without the log book, but the Court held that this would not have been a sale in the ordinary course of business of a mercantile agent and therefore the sale without the log book would have been outside the Factors Acts; it followed that the sale with the log book, where the log book had been obtained without the owner's consent, was also outside the Act.

An important decision on s. 9 of the Factors Act and s. 25(1) of the Sale of Goods Act 1979 is *National Employer's Insurance v. Jones* (1988)[38]. In that case a car was stolen and sold to A who sold it to B who in turn sold it to a car dealer C, who sold it to another car dealer D, who sold it to the defendant who bought it in good faith. It has been assumed in many previous transactions that in such circumstances the defendant was not protected since the original invalidity arising from the theft was not cured by any of the subsequent sales. However, in this case the defendant argued that the transaction fell within the literal scope of s. 9 because D had obtained possession of the goods with the consent of the dealer who had sold the goods to him and who was certainly a mercantile agent. It is true that both s. 9 and s. 25 talk about consent of the *seller* and not consent of the *owner* and Sir Denys Buckley in the Court of Appeal dissented from the majority view and held that the transaction was covered by s. 9 and s. 25. However, the majority of the Court of Appeal and a unanimous House of Lords took the opposite view. They held that the word 'seller' in s. 9 and s. 25 must be given a special meaning and could not cover a seller whose possession could be traced back through however many transactions to the unlawful possession of a thief. This must be correct since otherwise the sale by the thief to the first purchaser would not be protected, but the sale by that purchaser to the second purchaser would.

---

[37] [1951] 1 K.B. 275.
[38] [1990] A.C. 24.

Hire Purchase Act 1964 Part III

It would be seen that in modern times the vast majority of cases **6-35** which involve the operation of the *nemo dat* principle involve a dishonest handling of motor cars. This is no doubt because:

(a) a car is by nature easily moved; and

(b) cars command a ready cash price on the secondhand market and can in practice often be traced by the original owner.

One of the most common forms of dishonesty is for a person to acquire a car on hire-purchase terms and then to dispose of it for cash before he or she has completed the hire-purchase contract. In practice, he or she will find it difficult to dispose of the car for cash to an honest dealer because the existence of the hire-purchase transaction would normally be discovered by reference by the dealer to H.P.I. as discussed earlier. However, it is in practice very easy for a person who has acquired a car on hire-purchase to sell it for cash on the secondhand market by advertising, and equally very difficult for someone buying from him or her to know that the seller is not in fact the owner of the goods. Such transactions are not protected by s. 25 because someone acquiring goods on hire-purchase is not a buyer, nor by the Factors Act because the seller is not a mercantile agent.

In order to deal with this situation, the Hire Purchase Act of 1964 **6-36** created a new exception to the *nemo dat* rule by providing that if a car which was subject to a hire-purchase or credit sale agreement was sold to a private purchaser, that purchaser would acquire a good title if he or she bought it in good faith and without notice of the hire-purchase or credit sale agreement.

This protection is accorded only to private purchasers and does not apply to dealers. However, the private purchaser does not need to be the person who actually buys and makes the initial purchase of the goods from the person who is dishonestly disposing of goods. So, if X has a car on hire-purchase terms and dishonestly sells it to a dealer B who then sells it to C who buys it in good faith, not knowing of the defects in A's or B's title, then C will obtain a good title, even though he has bought from B the dealer and not from A the original hirer and even though B himself did not obtain a good title.

It is obviously very important therefore to know who is a 'private purchaser'. Private purchasers are those who are not 'trade or finance purchasers', and a trade or finance purchaser is one who at the time of the disposition carried on a business which consisted wholly or partly either of:

(a) purchasing motor vehicles for the purpose of offering or exposing them for sale; or

(b) providing finance by purchasing motor vehicles for the purpose of letting them under hire-purchase agreements or agreeing to sell them under conditional sale agreements.

It is perfectly possible to carry on either of these activities part time, so that someone who buys and sells cars as a sideline will be a trade purchaser, if he or she is doing it as a business; that is, with a view to making a profit. On the other hand, a company which is not in the motor trade or the financing of motor purchase business will be a private purchaser for the purpose of Part III of the 1964 Act.

CHAPTER 7

NON-EXISTENT GOODS, RISK AND FRUSTRATION

Suppose that the goods which are the subject of the contract never existed or once existed and have now ceased to exist, or that, the goods, although they exist, have been damaged or that goods of this kind are no longer available on the market, how does this affect the rights of the parties? There are two separate doctrines which are used to answer questions such as this. These are the doctrines of risk and of frustration. Before we examine these doctrines, however, we must consider the special case of goods which never existed at all or which, having once existed, have perished.

1 NON-EXISTENT GOODS

Section 6 of the Sale of Goods Act 1979 provides: **7-01**

'Where there is a contract for the sale of specific goods and the goods without the knowledge of the seller have perished at the time when the contract was made, the contract is void.'

This section is commonly assumed to have been an attempt by the draughtsman of the 1893 Act to state the effect of the famous pre-Act case of *Couturier v. Hastie* (1856)[1]. In that case the contract was for the sale of a specific cargo of corn which was on board a named ship sailing from Salonica to London. In fact, at the time the contract was made, the cargo of corn had been sold by the master of the ship in Tunis because it was fermenting owing to storm damage. (The master of the ship was of course the servant of the ship owners and not of the seller.) One might have expected that if on these facts litigation took place at all, it would arise by the buyer suing the seller for non-delivery of the goods. In fact, however, the seller sued the buyer, claiming that he was entitled to the price even though he had no goods to deliver. At first sight this seems an absurd argument since normally the buyer's obligation to pay the price is conditional on the seller being able to deliver the goods. The seller's argument was that in a contract of this kind the buyer had agreed to pay against delivery of the shipping documents which would have given him rights against the carriers and against the insurers of the

---

[1] (1856) 5 H.L.C. 673.

goods. As we shall see, this argument would sometimes succeed because of the rules about the passing of risk where the goods perished after the contract was made. Indeed, in some cases of international sales it would even succeed where the goods were *damaged* (as opposed to having perished) after shipment, but before the contract was made, because of the possibility that risk might retrospectively go back to the date of shipment. However, the Court of Exchequer Chamber and the House of Lords were agreed that in this case the seller's action failed.

7-02   *Couturier v. Hastie* has been extensively discussed, not only in relation to the law of sales, but also in relation to the general law of contract. It has been taken by some as an example of a general principle that if the parties' agreement is based on some shared fundamental mistake, then the contract is void. Other writers have treated it as an example of an overlapping but rather narrower principle that if, unknown to the parties, the subject matter of the contract does not exist or has ceased to exist, then the contract is void. The controversy as to whether either or both of these principles is part of the general law of contract has not been finally resolved and cannot be pursued in detail here. It is important to note however that s. 6 of the Sale of Goods Act 1979 does not turn on either of these principles.

In order to apply s. 6 one needs to know what is meant by the goods having *perished*. It is clear that in *Couturier v. Hastie* the corn may still have existed at the time of the contract. There is no evidence in the report of the case of what happened to the corn after it was sold in Tunis. It seems clear that it was treated as having perished because as a commercial entity the cargo had ceased to exist. In *Barrow, Lane and Ballard Ltd. v. Philip Phillips & Co. Ltd.* (1929)[2], there was a contract for 700 bags of ground nuts which were believed to be in a warehouse. In fact, unknown to the parties, 109 bags had been stolen before the contract was made. It was held that s. 6 applied and the contract was void. It will be seen that only some 15% of the contract parcel had been stolen, but this was treated as sufficient to destroy the parcel as a whole. Clearly, whether this will be so will depend very much on the particular facts of the case and precisely what it is the seller has contracted to deliver. It was probably also relevant that there was no realistic chance of recovering the stolen bags.

Goods will not be treated as having perished merely because they have been damaged. On the other hand there may be damage so extensive as effectively to deprive the goods of the commercial character under which they were sold. So in *Asfar & Co. Ltd. v. Blundell* (1896)[3], the

---

2   [1929] 1 K.B. 574.
3   [1896] 1 Q.B. 123.

contract was for a sale of a cargo of dates. The dates had become contaminated with sewage and had begun to ferment. Although all the dates were still available, the cargo was treated as commercially perished.

It will be seen that s. 6 only applies to the sale of specific goods and only applies where the goods have perished 'without the knowledge of the seller'. A seller who knows that the goods have perished will therefore normally be liable for breach of contract and might, in some cases, alternatively be liable for fraud. A difficult question is what the position would be if the seller ought to have known that the goods had perished. In 1856 communications between Tunis and London were no doubt not such as to make it easy for the seller to have discovered quickly what had happened to the cargo. This would not be the case today. The literal wording of s. 6 suggests that if the seller does not know that the goods have perished, even though he or she could easily have discovered it, the contract is void. It does not follow, however, that the buyer would be without a remedy since in some such cases the seller would be liable for having represented negligently that the goods did exist. This is one of the possible explanations of the famous Australian decision of *McRae v. Commonwealth Disposals Commission* (1951)[4], although this was actually a case where the goods had never existed rather than one where the goods had once existed and perished. In *McRae*, the Commonwealth Disposals Commission sold to the plaintiff the wreck of a ship which was said to be on a named reef off the coast of New Guinea. The plaintiff mounted an expedition to salvage the ship, only to find that the ship, and indeed the named reef, did not exist. It is easy to see that simply to hold on these facts that there was no contract would have been very unfair on the plaintiff who had wasted much time and money searching for a ship which did not exist. It was not surprising therefore that the High Court of Australia held that the plaintiff could recover this lost expenditure although they did not recover the profit they might have made if the ship had been there and had been successfully salvaged. It has been much discussed whether an English court would reach the same result. The Australian court took the view that s. 6 did not apply to the facts since it dealt only with goods which had once existed and had perished and not with goods that had never existed at all. Some commentators in England, however, have taken the view that s. 6 is simply a partial statement of the common law rule and that the common law rule applies not only to goods which are perished but also to goods which have never existed. It would be possible to accept this view but to hold that a seller could be sued for misrepresentation whether the goods perished or had never existed, if it could be shown either that he or she knew that the goods no longer existed or that he ought to have known this. In *McRae* the High

---

4   (1951) 84 C.L.R. 377.

Court of Australia would have held the sellers negligent but in 1951 it was widely believed that there was no liability to pay damages for loss caused by negligent misrepresentation; this is now clearly no longer the case since the decision of the House of Lords in *Hedley Byrne & Co. Ltd. v. Heller & Partners Ltd.* (1964)[5].

An alternative approach would be to say that except for those cases which are covered by the express words of s. 6 there is no rigid rule that simply because the goods do not exist there is no contract. Obviously, in many cases the rational inference will be that the parties' agreement is conditional upon the goods existing. In other cases (and this was the reasoning of the High Court of Australia in *McRae*), the seller may reasonably be treated as having contracted that the goods do exist. Yet a third possibility is that the buyer may have contracted on the basis that he or she would take the risk that the goods did exist (this was in effect the argument of the sellers in *Couturier v. Hastie*, rejected on the facts of that case but not necessarily to be rejected as never capable of arising).

2   THE DOCTRINE OF RISK[6]

7-04   The previous section was concerned with problems which arise where the goods have 'perished' before the contract is made. Obviously the goods may be destroyed or damaged after the contract is made. The principal tool used to allocate the loss which arises where the goods are damaged or destroyed after the contract is made is the doctrine of risk. This is a special doctrine developed for the law of sale, unlike the doctrine of frustration which is a general doctrine of the law of contract and which will be discussed in the next section.

What is the effect of the passing of risk?

7-05   It is important to emphasise that the doctrine of risk does not operate to bring the contract of sale to an end. It may, however, release one party from his or her obligations under the contract. So, for instance, if the goods are at the seller's risk and they are damaged or destroyed, this would in effect release the buyer from his or her obligation to accept the goods, but it would not release the seller from the obligation to deliver them. Conversely, if the goods are at the buyer's risk and are damaged or destroyed he or she may still be liable to pay the price even though the seller is no longer liable for not delivering the goods. In some cases

---

5   [1964] A.C. 465.
6   Sealy [1972B] C.L.J. 225.

where the goods are damaged this would be the fault of a third party and that third party may be liable to be sued. This is particularly likely to be the case where the goods are being carried because experience shows that goods in transit are particularly vulnerable to accidents. However, a very important practical consideration to take into account here is that a party will not necessarily have a tort action for damage to the goods simply because the risk as between buyer and seller has been placed on it[7]. This is because tort actions for damage to goods by third parties are usually only available to those who either own the goods or are in possession of them at the time that the damage is caused. So, if the goods are in the hands of the carrier in a situation where they still belong to the seller, but risk has been transferred to the buyer and the carrier carelessly damages the goods, the buyer will not normally have an action against the carrier. This is what happened to the buyer in *Leigh and Sillivan v. Aliakmon Shipping Co.* (1986)[8].

It follows from this, of course, that a very important practical consequence of the passing of risk is to determine which party needs to insure. If the parties are making a special agreement about risk, it will obviously be sensible to make an agreement which naturally fits in with the parties' standard insurance arrangements. So, if goods are delivered to the buyer on terms that it is not to become the owner until it has paid for them, it may still be sensible for the parties to agree that the risk is to pass to the buyer on delivery to it since once the goods are in the buyer's hands they will fall within the scope of the contents insurance of the buyer for its house, factory or office. A trap for the unwary here, however, may be that the contents insurance only covers those goods which are owned by the insured. Such provisions are quite common in insurance policies and the prudent insured should take steps to make certain that goods which are in its possession but which it does not yet own, are insured.

When does risk pass?

The basic rule is set out in s. 20 of the Sale of Goods Act 1979 which provides:

> '(1)   Unless otherwise agreed, the goods remain at the seller's risk until the property in them is transferred to the buyer, but when the property in them is transferred to the buyer the goods are at the buyer's risk whether delivery has been made or not.

7-06

---

7   In certain circumstances a buyer who receives the Bill of Lading will have a contract action against the carrier but the details of this possibility are outside the scope of this work.

8   [1986] 2 W.L.R. 902.

(2)   But where delivery has been delayed through the fault of either buyer or seller the goods are at the risk of the party at fault as regards any loss which might not have occurred but for such fault.

(3)   Nothing in this section affects the duties or liabilities of either seller or buyer as a bailee or custodier of the goods of the other party.'

It will be seen that English law has adopted the basic rule that risk is to pass at the same time as property. This is perhaps the most important example of the general principle discussed in Chapter 6 that the passing of property is most significant, not for itself, but for the consequences which flow from it. The basic rule automatically takes care of all the problems just discussed of who can sue a third party who negligently damages the goods and of insuring goods which one does not own.

Nevertheless, it is quite clear that the parties can and frequently do separate the passing of risk and property. So, in standard conditions of sale the seller will often provide that risk is to pass on delivery but that property is not to pass until the goods have been paid for. This is because the seller does not wish to be bothered with insuring the goods once he or she has delivered them, but is anxious to retain ownership of the goods as security against not being paid in full.

In the same way, the basic rule may be modified by commercial practice. So, in the most common form of international sale of goods, the cif contract (cost, insurance, freight), the usual understanding will be that risk is to pass as from the date of shipment of the goods, but commonly property will not pass until the seller has tendered the documents (usually the bill of lading, invoice and policy of insurance) and been paid. This is because the most common practice is for the seller to retain the shipping documents (and indeed to take the bill of lading to his or her own order) to ensure that he or she gets paid. The rule that the risk passes as from shipment means that the buyer has to look in respect of damage after shipment to its rights under the policy of insurance or against the carrier. In the normal case the buyer will be protected as against the carrier because it will receive the bill of lading and in most cases the transfer of the bill transfers the seller's contract rights against the carrier under the bill of lading to the buyer. This did not happen in *Leigh and Sillivan v. Aliakmon* above, because in that case the parties had made special arrangements which did not involve the transfer of the bill of lading and had not adequately addressed their minds in making these arrangements to the problems of suing the carrier. We may also note in passing that in a cif contract risk may, and quite often does, pass before the contract has been made because of the presumption that risk passes as from shipment. This means that if the goods are sold while they are on the high seas, the risk of damage between shipment and the date of contract will pass to the buyer. This rule did not apply in *Couturier v. Hastie* because the goods in that case had not simply been damaged but had totally perished[9].

These cases can no doubt be explained on the basis of an implied agreement between the parties. The risk is to pass in accordance with what is commercially usual. There seem, however, to be at least two kinds of cases where risk may pass at a different time from property even though there is no expressed or implied agreement. The first arises in the case of sales of unascertained goods. As we have seen, property cannot pass in such a case until the goods are ascertained. However, there may be cases where property is not ascertained because the goods form part of an unascertained bulk, but nevertheless fairness requires that risk should pass. The classic example is *Sterns v. Vickers* (1923)[10], in this case the sellers had some 200,000 gallons of white spirit in a tank belonging to a storage company. They sold to the buyers some 120,000 gallons of the spirit and gave the buyers a delivery warrant. The effect of the delivery warrant was that the storage company undertook to deliver the white spirit to the buyers or as the buyers might order. In fact the buyers sub-sold, but the sub-purchaser did not wish to take possession of the spirit at once and arranged with the storage company to store it on his behalf, paying rent for the storage. Clearly, although there had been a sale and a sub-sale, ownership was still in the hands of the original sellers since the goods were still unascertained. While the bulk was unseparated, the spirit deteriorated. The Court of Appeal held that although there was no agreement between the parties, the risk had passed as between the original seller and buyer to the buyer. The reason for this was that as soon as the buyers had the delivery warrant, they were immediately able to obtain delivery of the spirit and therefore risk should pass to them even though they chose not to take immediate possession of the goods.

The facts of *Stern v. Vickers* are rather special since the reason why property did not pass to the buyer was a deliberate decision by the buyer. It does not always follow that risk will pass before the goods are ascertained; indeed the usual rule must be to the contrary. So in *Healy v. Howlett* (1917)[11], the plaintiff was an Irish fish exporter. He consigned to an Irish railway 190 boxes of mackerel which would be sent to England to perform three contracts. The plaintiff had sold 20 boxes to the defendant, a Billingsgate fish merchant, and sent a telegram to Holyhead telling the railway officials to deliver 20 of the boxes to the defendant

---

9　See *C. Groom v. Barber* [1915] 1 K.B. 316; *Manbre Saccharine Co. Ltd. v. Corn Products Co. Ltd.* [1919] 1 K.B. 198.

10　[1923] 1 K.B. 78.

11　[1917] 1 K.B. 337.

and the other boxes to the other buyers. No specific box was appropriated to any specific sale. Unfortunately, the train was delayed and the fish deteriorated before they reached Holyhead. It was held that as property had not passed to the buyer since the goods were not ascertained, equally risk had not passed to the buyer, because there was nothing in the circumstances to justify departure from the *prima facie* rule that risk passes at the same time as property.

7-08   The second situation, where it is usually assumed that risk does not pass even though property may have passed, is illustrated by the pre-Act case of *Head v. Tattersall* (1870)[12], which it is generally assumed would be decided in the same way after the Act. In this case the plaintiff bought a horse from the defendant who warranted that it had been hunted with the Bicester hounds. The contract provided that the horse might be returned by a certain day if it appeared that it had not in fact been hunted with the Bicester hounds. The horse had in fact not been hunted with the hounds and the plaintiff chose to return it before the agreed date. On the face of it the plaintiff was clearly entitled to do this, but before the horse had been returned it had been injured while in the plaintiff's possession, although without any fault on his part. The defendant argued that the correct way to analyse the situation was to treat the property as having passed from the defendant to the plaintiff subject to an agreement that it might revest in the defendant at a later stage, but subject to a proviso that the horse was at the plaintiff's risk while it was in his hands. The court held, however, that the plaintiff was entitled to return the horse. This can only be on the basis that the agreement that the horse might be returned was an agreement which was unqualified, but it would often be the case that it would be a more sensible interpretation of an agreement of this kind that the goods should be returned only if they were in substantially the same condition when returned as when originally delivered.

The general rule stated in s. 20(1) of the Sale of Goods Act 1979 is subject to the qualifications contained in sub-sections (2) and (3). Sub-section (2) means that if the seller is late in making the delivery or the buyer is late in accepting delivery, this may mean that the incidence of risk is different from what it would otherwise have been. This would be so, however, only if the loss is one which might not have occurred if delivery had not been delayed. However, the onus will be on the party who is in delay to show that the loss would have happened in any event[13]. Sub-section (3) is really no more than a specific example of the general principle that the passing of risk is to do with the allocation of

---

[12] (1870) L.R. 7 Ex. 7.
[13] See *Demby Hamilton Ltd. v. Barden* [1949] 1 All E.R. 435.

the risk of damage which is not the fault of either party. The most important example of this is where the risk is on one party, but the other party is in possession of the goods and fails to take good care of them.

We should also note s. 33 of the Sale of Goods Act 1979 which provides: **7-09**

'Where the seller of goods agrees to deliver them at his own risk at a place other than that where they are when sold, the buyer must nevertheless (unless otherwise agreed) take any risk of deterioration in the goods necessarily incident to the course of transit.'

Practical examples of the application of this section are very hard to find. It seems probable that the draftsman had in mind a pre-Act case in which goods were sent by canal barge and the court held that some risk of splashing by water was a necessary incident of this form of transit. So s. 33 would not apply to a case where the goods deteriorated because they were not fit to undertake the journey which had been contracted for. So in *Mash and Murrell v. Joseph I Emanuel Ltd.* (1961)[14], potatoes were consigned from Cyprus to Liverpool and it was held that not only must the potatoes be sound when loaded, but they were also impliedly warranted sound enough to survive the ordinary risks of sea carriage from Cyprus to Liverpool. The result would be different if the potatoes had gone off because they had been inadequately ventilated during the voyage, because that would be a risk which as between seller and buyer, was on the buyer (although of course the buyer might have a claim against the carrier).

3 THE DOCTRINE OF FRUSTRATION

The doctrine of frustration is part of the general law of contract. It   **7-10** provides that in certain exceptional circumstances events which take place after the contract may be so cataclysmic in effect that it is appropriate to treat them as bringing the contract to an end. In practice, the operation of the doctrine is limited to events which make it physically or legally impossible to perform the contract or changes of circumstance so great that in effect the continued performance of the contract would be to require the performance of what is commercially a fundamentally different contract. It is quite clear that the mere fact that the changes of circumstance made it more difficult or more expensive for one of the parties to perform the contract is not enough. In principle there can be no doubt that this doctrine applies to contracts for the sale of goods like any other contract.

---

14   [1961] 1 All E.R. 485; [1962] 1 All E.R. 77.

When does the doctrine of frustration apply?

7-11   Section 7 of the Act contains a provision which deals expressly with frustration, this provides:

> 'Where there is an agreement to sell specific goods and subsequently the goods, without any fault on the part of the seller or buyer, perish before the risk passes to the buyer, the agreement is avoided.'

This section is clearly a very incomplete statement of the doctrine of frustration as applied to contracts of sale. It deals only with specific goods and it deals only with goods which perish, whereas frustration may involve many other events than the destruction of the goods. For instance, where goods are sold internationally, there is often a requirement to obtain an export or import licence. Failure to obtain such a licence would not normally be a frustrating event because the parties would know at the time of the contract that the licence was required and the contract would often expressly or impliedly require one of the parties to obtain (or at least to use his or her best endeavours to obtain) the licence. However, it might be that after the contract was made, a Government introduced a wholly new export or import licensing system which was unforeseen. There might be plausible arguments in such a case that the contract was frustrated.

7-12   It is also possible to argue that a contract for the sale of unascertained goods is frustrated, but of course such goods cannot usually perish (except for the special case of sale of part of a bulk as discussed below). In practice the courts, although admitting the possibility that sales of unascertained goods can be frustrated, have been very slow in fact to hold them frustrated. Two examples of unsuccessful arguments will perhaps illustrate this point. In *Blackburn Bobbin Ltd. v. T W Allen Ltd.* (1918)[15], there was a contract for the sale of 70 standards of Finland birch timber. Unknown to the buyer the seller intended to load the timber in Finland for shipment to England. This was the usual trade practice at the time of the contract. In fact before delivery began the 1914 war broke out and shipment became impossible. It was held that the contract was not frustrated. It will be seen that although the contract called for timber from Finland, it did not contain any provision that the timber was to be in Finland at the time of the contract. This illustrates the fundamental point that whether frustration applies or not always depends on the precise nature of the contractual obligations undertaken and the precise nature of the calamity which has overtaken them. A second case is *Tsakiroglou & Co. Ltd. v. Noblee and Thorl* (1962)[16]. This was one of a

---

15   [1918] 1 K.B. 540; [1918] 2 K.B. 467.
16   [1962] A.C. 93.

number of contracts in which Sudanese ground nuts had been sold cif European ports. At the time of the contract the seller, whose duty it is under a cif contract to arrange and pay for the sea carriage to the port of destination, intended to put the goods on a ship going through the Suez Canal. By the time the date for shipment arrived, the canal was closed because of the 1956 Suez Crisis. In order to perform the contract therefore, the seller needed to put the ground nuts on a ship coming to Europe via the Cape of Good Hope. This was perfectly possible since the cargo was not perishable, but involved the seller in significant extra expenditure, partly because the route via the Cape was much longer and partly because the closure of the Canal had in any event greatly increased world freight rates by altering the balance between supply and demand for shipping space. The seller argued that these changes were so dramatic as to frustrate the contract. This was not at all an implausible argument and one experienced judge, McNair J, in a case on virtually identical facts, did hold that the contract was frustrated. However, the House of Lords in this case held that the contract was not frustrated. The principal reason for this decision seems to be that in a cif contract the seller includes the cost of carriage as an integral part of the agreement. The seller therefore takes the risk of freight rates going up and the benefit of freight rates going down. The shipping market is volatile and freight rates go up and down all the time. What had happened was simply an extreme example of price fluctuation, but that by itself was not enough to bring the contract to an end.

Perhaps the most interesting cases are two examples where farmers have sold in advance the product of a harvest and then suffered an unforeseen bad harvest which has produced a crop much less than anticipated.

In *Howell v. Coupland* (1876) [17], a farmer sold in March for delivery upon harvesting the following autumn, 200 tons of potatoes to come from his farm. In fact only 80 tons were harvested. The buyer accepted delivery of the 80 tons and brought an action for damages for non-delivery of the balance of 120 tons. It was held that the unforeseen potato blight which had affected the crop released the seller from his obligation to deliver any more than had in fact been grown. It should be noted that in fact the buyer was perfectly happy to accept and pay for the 80 tons; it was certainly arguable that if the potato blight released the seller, it also released the buyer from any obligation to take the potatoes at all. Obviously there could be commercial situations in which if the buyer could not obtain the full 200 tons from one source, it was perfectly reasonable of him to refuse to accept any delivery at all. The case does

7-13

---

[17] (1876) 1 Q.B.D. 258.

not decide that a buyer could not elect to do this. (Section 7 of the Sale of Goods Act is usually thought to be an attempt by the draftsman to state the effects of *Howell v. Coupland*, but it is usually held that s. 7 does not in fact cover the case since the goods in *Howell v. Coupland* were not specific, but rather future goods. Nevertheless it is usually assumed that *Howell v. Coupland* was correctly decided and would be decided the same way today.)

In the modern case of *H R & S Sainsbury Ltd. v. Street* (1972)[18], the farmer contracted to sell to a corn merchant 275 tons of barley to be grown on his farm. In this case there was a generally poor harvest and only 140 tons were harvested on the defendant's farm. The defendant argued that the contract was frustrated and sold the 140 tons to another merchant. (The reason no doubt being that because of the generally poor harvest, barley prices were higher than expected and the defendant was then able to get a better price from another merchant.) McKenna J held that the farmer was in breach of contract by not delivering the 140 tons which had actually been harvested, although the bad harvest did relieve him of any obligation to deliver the balance of 135 tons. Again, it should be noted that in this case the buyer was willing and indeed anxious to take the 140 tons and the case does not therefore decide that the buyer in such a case was bound to take the 140 tons, although the doctrine of frustration where it operates, does normally operate to release both parties from future performance of the contract.

In the cases above, the farmer appears to have sold his crop in advance to a single merchant. Obviously, a farmer might expect to harvest 200 tons and agree to sell 100 tons off his farm to each of two different merchants. Suppose in such a case he had a crop of only 150 tons? It is unclear what the effect of this would be. Commentators have usually argued that in this case the fair result would be that each of the buyers should have 75 tons, but it is unclear whether this result can be reached. A similar problem arises where a seller has a bulk cargo, say 1,000 tons of wheat on board a known ship and sells 500 tons to A and 500 tons to B, only for it to be discovered on arrival that 100 tons of the cargo are damaged without any fault on the part of the seller.

The effect of frustration

If a frustrating event takes place, its effect is to bring the contract to an end at once and relieve both parties from any further obligation to perform the contract. This is so even though the frustrating event usually only makes it impossible for one party to perform. So the fact

---

[18]   [1972] 1 W.L.R. 834; [1972] 3 All E.R. 1127.

that the seller is unable to deliver the goods does not mean that the buyer is unable to pay the price, but the seller's inability to deliver the goods relieves the buyer of the obligation to pay the price. This rule is easy to apply where the contract is frustrated before either party has done anything to perform it, but the contract is often frustrated after some acts of performance have taken place. This has proved a surprisingly difficult question to resolve.

At common law it was eventually held in the leading case of *Fibrosa v. Fairbairn* (1943)[19], that if a buyer had paid in advance for the goods, he or she could recover the advance payment in full if no goods at all had been delivered before the contract was frustrated. However, that decision is based on a finding that there had been a 'total failure of consideration'; that is that the buyer had received no part of what it expected to receive under the contract. If there was a partial failure of consideration, that is if the buyer had received some of the goods, then it would not have been able to recover an advance payment of the price even though the advance payment was significantly greater than the value of the goods which it had received. This obviously appears unfair on the buyer. The decision in the *Fibrosa* case was also potentially unfair on the seller. Even though the seller has not delivered any goods before the contract is frustrated, it may well have incurred expenditure where the goods have to be manufactured for the buyer's requirements and some or perhaps even all of this expenditure may be wasted if the goods cannot easily be resold because the buyer's requirements are special. These defects in the law were largely remedied by the Law Reform (Frustrated Contracts) Act 1943 which gave the court a wide discretion to order repayment of prices which had been paid in advance or to award compensation to a seller who had incurred wasted expenditure before the contract was frustrated.

Section 2(5)(c) of the 1943 Act provides that the Act shall not apply to:

'Any contract to which Section 7 of the Sale of Goods Act ... applies or ... any other contract for the sale, or for the sale and delivery, of specific goods, where the contract is frustrated by reason of the fact that the goods have perished.'

So the 1943 Act does not apply to cases where the contract is frustrated either under s. 7 of the Sale of Goods Act or in other cases where it is frustrated by the goods perishing. (It should be mentioned here that it is not at all clear whether it is possible for the contract to be frustrated by perishing of the goods other than under s. 7. Some commentators have strongly argued for this view, but it has been

---

19   [1943] A.C. 32.

doubted by others and the question has never been tested in litigation.) On the other hand, the 1943 Act does apply where the contract is frustrated by any event other than the perishing of the goods. It is really quite unclear why Parliament drew this distinction, but the effect is that if the contract of sale is frustrated by the destruction of the goods, then the effects of frustration are determined by the common law before the 1943 Act with the results described above.

Force majeure clauses[20]

The English law doctrine of frustration is rather narrow in its scope and the parties may often wish therefore to provide for unexpected contingencies which do not or may not fall within the doctrine of frustration. Such clauses in commercial contracts are very common. They are often referred to as *force majeure* clauses, *force majeure* being the equivalent, though rather wider French doctrine akin to frustration.

There is no doubt that the parties are free to widen the effect of unexpected events in this way, indeed the rationale commonly put forward for the narrow scope of the doctrine of frustration is exactly that the parties can widen their provision if they choose to do so. It is not possible here to consider all the clauses which might possibly be found, which would justify a book in itself. Sometimes clauses are found which simply say that the contract is subject to *force majeure*, but this is probably a bad practice since it is far from certain exactly what an English court will hold *force majeure* to mean. More sophisticated clauses usually therefore set out what is meant either by a list of events such as strikes, lockouts, bad weather and so on, or by a general provision that the events must be unforeseen and outside the control of the parties, or by some combination of these. A typical clause will also frequently require the party (usually the seller) who claims that there has been *force majeure*, to give prompt notice to the buyer. Whereas the doctrine of frustration always brings the contract to an end, *force majeure* clauses often opt for less drastic consequences. So it may be provided that if there is a strike which affects delivery, the seller is to be given extra time, though the clause may go on to say that if the interruption is sufficiently extended, the seller is to be relieved altogether.

---

[20] See *Force Majeure and Frustration of Contract*, ed. Ewan McKendrick (Lloyds of London, 1991) especially Chapters 1, 2, 3, 10 and 12.

CHAPTER 8

DEFECTIVE GOODS

1 INTRODUCTION

This chapter is concerned with the legal problems which arise   **8-01**
where the goods are 'defective'. (The word defective is put in
quotation marks because what we mean by saying that the goods are
defective is itself one of the central questions to be discussed.) It may
be safely suggested that complaints about the quality of the goods far
exceed in number any of the other complaints which may be made
where goods are bought, so the topic is of great practical importance. It
is also of some considerable theoretical complexity because of the way
in which the rules have developed. Liability for defective goods may
be either contractual, tortious or criminal. The main part of this
chapter will be devoted to considering the situations in which the
buyer has a contractual remedy against the seller on the grounds that
the goods are not as the seller contracted. However, liability for
defective goods may also be based on the law of tort. Since 1932 it has
been clear that in most cases there will be liability in tort where
someone suffers personal injury or damage to his or her property
arising from the defendant having negligently put goods into
circulation. This liability does not depend on there being any contract
between plaintiff and defendant, though the possibility of such a claim
is not excluded by the fact that there is a contract between plaintiff and
defendant. So a buyer of a motor car might formulate the claim against
the seller in this way on the basis that the seller had negligently carried
out the pre-delivery inspection. In practice, the buyer would usually
be better off to pursue his or her contractual rights against the seller
but this will not always be so. A major development in tort liability has
taken place since the adoption in 1985 by the European Community of
a directive on product liability, enacted into English law by Part I of
the Consumer Protection Act 1987. This Act is aimed at imposing
liability for defective products on producers of products but sellers
may be producers either where their distribution is vertically
integrated so that the same company is manufacturing, marketing and
distributing the goods retail, or, where although they are not
manufacturing the goods, they sell them as if they were theirs (as in
the case of major stores which sell 'own brand' goods).

8-02   A seller may also come under criminal liability. A typical, and all too common example, is the second hand car dealer who turns back the odometer so as to make it appear that the secondhand car has covered less miles than is in fact the case. This is a criminal offence under the Trade Description Act. The notion of using the criminal law to regulate the activities of dishonest sellers is very old and goes back to the medieval imposition of standard weights and measures. However, the modern development of an effective consumer lobby has greatly increased the scope of criminal law in this area. In many cases, where there is criminal liability, there would also be civil liability either in contract or in tort. So the buyer of the secondhand car with the odometer fraudulently turned back would, in virtually all cases, have a civil claim either on the basis that the seller had contracted that the mileage was genuine or on the basis that the seller had fraudulently or negligently represented that it was genuine. Many buyers, however, would find that seeking to enforce this remedy would be a forbidding task because of the expense and trauma involved. The great advantage of enforcement through criminal law is that it is in the hands of local authority officials (commonly called Trading Standards Officers) whose job it is to enforce the criminal law in this area and the cost of whose time falls upon the general body of tax payers and not upon individual victims of undesirable trading practices. (The disadvantage is that the criminal law primarily operates by punishing the guilty rather than by ordering them to compensate the victim.)

8-03   Two other preliminary points may be made. The first is that a seller may seek to exclude or limit his or her liability by inserting appropriate words into the contract of sale. Historically, this has been an extremely common practice and indeed it still is. However, the modern tendency has been to regard such clauses with considerable hostility and, particularly in consumer transactions, they are now very likely to be ineffective. The rules relating to exclusion clauses are discussed in Chapter 9. The second point is that this chapter is concerned to set out the duties of the seller and manufacturer. In practice, the duties of the seller are intimately connected with the remedies of the buyer. In particular it is of critical importance whether failure by the seller to deliver goods of the right quality entitles the buyer to reject the goods (that is to refuse to accept them) or simply to give him or her a right to damages. In practice, the rules about the seller's obligations and the buyer's remedies interact, because sometimes courts are reluctant to hold that goods are defective where the result would be to entitle the buyer to reject them even though they would be content for the buyer to have a less drastic remedy by way of damages. The remedies of the parties are considered more fully in Chapter 10.

2 LIABILITY IN CONTRACT: EXPRESS TERMS

Two hundred years ago, English law in this area was more or less accurately represented by the maxim *caveat emptor* (let the buyer beware). Under this regime the seller was only liable insofar as he or she had expressly made undertakings about the goods. As we shall see, this is quite clearly no longer the case and English law has come to impose quite extensive liabilities on the seller even where he or she makes no express undertakings by holding that the contract is subject to the implied terms discussed later. Nevertheless, the possibility of express terms is still very important. In any complex commercial contract where goods are being procured for the buyer's specific requirements, the buyer would be well-advised to formulate very carefully the express undertakings which he or she wishes the seller to make. Even in commercial dealings, however, where goods have been bought 'off the shelf' not much may be said by way of express undertakings.

It might be thought to be a relatively simple task to decide whether or not a seller has made express undertakings about the goods. In fact, this is not the case and English law has managed to make this a much more difficult question than it would appear at first sight. The problems can be illustrated by the decision of the Court of Appeal in *Oscar Chess v. Williams* (1957)[1]. In this case, the seller wished to trade in his existing car in part-exchange for a newer car. The buyer, who was a dealer, asked him how old the car was, and the seller described it as a 1948 Morris. In fact the car was a 1939 Morris but the 1939 and 1948 models were identical and the log book had been altered by a previous owner so as to make the car appear to be a 1948 model. At this time, 1948 cars commanded a higher trade-in price than 1939 cars and the dealer allowed the seller a price in the 1948 range. In due course, the dealer became suspicious and checked the cylinder block number with Cowley, which showed that the car was a 1939 car. There was no doubt on the evidence that the seller had stated that the car was a 1948 model, but the majority of the Court of Appeal held that he had not contracted that it was a 1948 model.

Why did the court reach this decision? The theoretical test is usually formulated by asking what the parties intended. How did the Court of Appeal discover what the parties had intended? Of course, if the parties had said what they intended, this test would be easy to apply but more often than not, the parties do not say what they intend. In practice, if the parties express no intention, the court is in effect substituting its own view of what the parties, as reasonable people, probably intended. This

---

1   [1957] 1 All E.R. 325; [1957] 1 W.L.R. 370.

is necessarily a vague and flexible test. Over the years a number of factors have been taken into account. One argument would be that the statement was of a trivial commendatory nature such that no one should be expected to treat it as meant to be contractually binding. Classic examples would be the house described by an estate agent as 'a desirable residence' or an obviously secondhand car described by a car dealer as 'as good as new'. It is probably fair to say that modern courts are less willing to accept this classification in marginal cases, particularly where the buyer is a consumer. So, in *Andrews v. Hopkinson* (1957)[2], a car dealer described a secondhand car as 'it's a good little bus. I would stake my life on it'. This was held to be contractually binding and not merely a commendatory statement. (In fact the car when sold had a badly defective steering mechanism, and a week after being delivered suddenly swerved into a lorry.)

8-05   The statement in *Oscar Chess v. Williams* as to the age of the car was clearly not in the blandly commendatory category. It was clearly an important statement and affected the price which was offered for the car. In the circumstances one would normally expect such statements to be contractually binding. The most important factor in the decision was probably that the seller was a consumer and the buyer was a dealer, a kind of reverse consumerism. It is very plausible to think that if the facts had been reversed and the seller had been a dealer, the result would have been different. This analysis is supported by the later decision of the Court of Appeal in *Bentley v. Harold Smith Motors* (1965)[3]. In this case the sellers, who were dealers, claimed to be experts in tracing the history of secondhand Bentley motor cars and assured the prospective buyer that a particular car had only done 20,000 miles since it had been fitted with a replacement engine and gear box. It was held that this statement was contractually binding. Another factor which distinguishes the *Oscar Chess* and *Bentley* cases is that in the *Bentley* case the sellers had held themselves out as capable of discovering the truth, and probably were, whereas in the *Oscar Chess* case, the seller was clearly not at fault since he had not unreasonably relied on the statement in the log book. It is quite clear, however, that the mere fact that a seller is not at fault does not mean that his or her statements are not contractually binding.

Another factor would be whether there was a significant time lag between the making of the statement and the completion of the contract. In *Routledge v. McKay* (1954)[4], both buyer and seller were private persons and the seller stated that a motorcycle he was offering was a 1942 model,

---

2   [1957] 1 Q.B. 229.
3   [1965] 2 All E.R. 65; [1965] 1 W.L.R. 623.
4   [1954] 1 All E.R. 855; [1954] 1 W.L.R. 615.

again relying on a statement in the log book which had been fraudulently altered by an earlier owner. The parties did not actually complete the contract until a week later, and it was held by the Court of Appeal that the statement as to the age of the motorcycle was not a contractual term. On the other hand, in the case of *Schawel v. Reade* (1913)[5], a potential buyer who was looking at a horse which he wished to use for stud purposes, started to examine it and was told by the seller 'you need not look for anything: the horse is perfectly sound'. The buyer stopped his examination and some three weeks later bought the horse which turned out to be unfit for stud purposes. In this case it was held that the statement as to the soundness of the horse was a term of the contract.

8-06

In the cases so far discussed, the contract was concluded by oral negotiations. Of course, the parties often render the contract into writing. Obviously, if they incorporate everything that is said in negotiations into the written contract, it will be clear that they intend it to be legally binding. But suppose an important statement is made in negotiations and is left out of the written contract. At one time it was believed that the so-called parol evidence rule meant that such statements did not form part of the contract. It is undoubtedly the law that the parties cannot give evidence of what was said in the negotiations for the purpose of helping the court interpret the contract they have actually made. (Of course the history of negotiations may be relevant to decide whether there was a contract at all.) This rule often surprises laymen and at first sight seems odd. Certainly many other legal systems do not have the same rule. However, it is clear that, if the parties have agreed on a written contract as a complete statement of what they intend, the exclusion of the earlier negotiations is perfectly rational because it is of the essence of negotiations that there is give and take and the parties change their position. Accordingly, what parties have said as a negotiating position earlier cannot be taken to be a safe guide as to what they intended in the complete written statement.

8-07

The above rule is well-established but its scope is, in practice, quite seriously restricted because courts are quite willing to entertain arguments that what looks like a complete written contract is not in fact a complete contract at all, but simply a partial statement of the contract. In fact the courts have recognised two different analyses here, though their practical effect is often the same. One analysis is to say that there is a contract partly in writing and partly oral; the other analysis is to say that there are two contracts, one in writing and one oral. The practical effect in both cases is to permit evidence to be given of oral statements

---

5   [1913] 2 I.R. 81.

which qualify, add to, or even contradict what is contained in the written contract. An excellent example of this is the case of *Evans v. Andrea Merzario* (1976)[6]. In this case the plaintiff was an engineering firm which commonly imported machinery from Italy. For this purpose it used the defendant as forwarding agent (that is, as a firm which organised the carriage of the goods, although it did not carry the goods itself). The transactions were carried out using the defendant's standard conditions which were based on the standard conditions of the forwarding trade. In 1967 the defendant decided to switch over to use of containers and a representative of the defendant called on the plaintiff to discuss this change. The plaintiff had always attached great importance to its goods being carried below deck because of the risk of corrosion by sea-spray while crossing the Channel. In conventional carriage of the kind used before 1967, goods would normally be in the hold and therefore clearly below the deck line. In a container ship, many of the goods are carried above the deck line because of the way the containers are stacked in the middle of the ship. This switch to containers therefore carried with it a greatly increased chance that the goods would be above deck and would be affected by spray. The defendant's representative assured the plaintiff that the goods would always be carried below deck. Several transactions followed, all of which were again on the defendant's standard conditions which purported to permit carriage above deck. On one particular voyage a container carrying goods belonging to the plaintiff and being well above deck, fell overboard and was lost. The plaintiff may have had an action against the carrier but this action would probably have been subject to limitations in the carrier's standard terms. The plaintiff therefore elected to sue the defendant which claimed that it was protected by the clause in its standard conditions that it could arrange for carriage of the containers above deck. The Court of Appeal was clear, however, that the defendant was not so protected. Two members of the Court of Appeal held that there was a single contract, partly in writing, partly oral; the third member held that there were in fact two contracts (this difference in analysis only seems to matter where there is some legal requirement that the contract should be in writing or where there have been attempts to transfer the rights of one of the parties and it may be arguable that the rights under the written contract may be transferred independently of a separate collateral contract).

8-08   It can be seen that the decision in the *Evans v. Andrea Merzario* case is very far-reaching. In effect, all the transactions between the parties were subject to the oral undertaking given by the representative in his 1967 visit, even years later when all the relevant personnel in the two

---

[6]   [1976] 1 All E.R. 930; [1976] 1 W.L.R. 1078.

companies concerned might well have changed. From the point of view of the defendants, this is not at all an attractive result. In practice, modern standard written contracts often contain clauses designed to reduce the possibility of this kind of reasoning by providing expressly that the written contract is the whole of the contract between the parties and that all previous negotiations are not binding unless expressly incorporated into the contract. Such 'merger' or 'whole contract' clauses are very common, but their legal effect does not seem to have been tested in litigation. It would probably be imprudent of sellers to assume that the presence of such a clause in their standard written terms would always prevent them from being bound by an oral statement made by one of their sales representatives.

3 LIABILITY FOR MISREPRESENTATION

Where the seller has made statements about the goods but the court has held that these statements are not terms of the contract it might be thought that this was the end of the matter. However, it is quite clear that this is not the case. Some such statements will give rise to liability in misrepresentation. **8-09**

What is a misrepresentation?

Basically a misrepresentation is a statement of a fact made by one party to the contract to the other party before the contract is made which induces that other party to enter into the contract but is not characterised as being a term of the contract. So the statement in *Oscar Chess v. Williams* that the car was a 1948 Morris was, if it was not a term of the contract, undoubtedly a misrepresentation. **8-10**

It should be noted, however, that not all of the terms of a contract are concerned with making statements of fact. Many terms contain promises as to future conduct, for example, that we will deliver the goods next week. In principle a promise to deliver goods next week is not capable of being a misrepresentation because it is not a statement of fact. For such a promise to give rise to liability it must be a term of the contract. This principle is well established but it is subject to one very important qualification. Hidden within many statements which look like statements of intention or opinion or undertakings as to the future there may be a statement of fact. This is because, as was said by Bowen LJ in *Edgington v. Fitzmaurice* (1885)[7] 'the state of a man's mind is as much a

---

7   (1885) 29 Ch. D. 459.

fact as the state of his digestion'. The application of this famous aphorism is well illustrated by that case in which a company issued a prospectus inviting members of the public to lend money to it and stating that the money would be employed so as to improve the buildings and extend the business. In fact the directors intended to spend the loan on discharging certain existing liabilities. It was held that the company had not contracted to spend the money on improving the buildings and extending the business but there had been a misrepresentation of fact because what the intention of the company was at the time of the prospectus was a question of fact. If the directors had in fact intended to spend the money on improving the buildings and extending the business and had later changed their minds then there would have been no liability in misrepresentation since there would have been no misstatement about the intention of the company at the time of the loan. On the other hand, of course, if the directors had contracted that the money would be spent in this way they would have broken the contract if they had later changed their minds.

8-11   In the same way a statement of opinion is a statement of fact about what one's opinion currently is. So if in *Oscar v. Williams* the seller had said that he thought that the car was a 1948 Morris he would not have been misrepresenting his state of mind since he did indeed think that it was. But if this had not in fact been his opinion then he would have been liable. So a car salesperson who is asked how many miles a car does to the gallon and says 'I don't know but I think about 40' when in fact he or she believes the mileage per gallon to be no better than 30 is guilty of misrepresenting his or her state of mind. Furthermore, courts have been prepared to hold that where people who state an opinion look as if they know what they are talking about, they may implicitly represent not only that they hold the opinion but that they know some facts upon which the opinion could reasonably be based. So, even if the car salesperson believes that the car will do 40 miles to the gallon, this may be a misrepresentation if he or she has never read any investigations. This is certainly the case where sales representatives are selling a particular brand of new car about which the customer could reasonably expect them to be well informed.

Sales representatives have a tendency to make eulogistic statements about the goods which they are trying to sell. Historically English law has recognised that not all such eulogistic statements should be treated as giving rise to liability on the grounds that no reasonable man would take them seriously. It is probably fair to say, however, that standards have risen in this area and that courts are significantly more likely today to hold that a statement is either a term or a misrepresentation. This will certainly be the case with eulogistic statements which purport to be backed up by facts and figures.

In order to create liability it is necessary to show not only that there has been a misrepresentation but that the other party to the contract entered into the contract because of the misrepresentation. So in a number of 19th century cases concerning flotation of companies, it was shown that there were fraudulent statements in the prospectus but it was also shown that some people bought shares in the company without ever having seen the prospectus and were ignorant of its contents. It was held that such a person could not rely on the undoubted misrepresentation in the prospectus. Even where one party knows there is misrepresentation he or she may not have entered into the contract because of it but may have relied on his or her own judgment or indeed known that the statement was untrue. On the other hand, it is not necessary to show that the misrepresentation was the only reason for entering into the contract. It would be sufficient to show that the misrepresentation was a significant reason for entering into the contract. Of course, people often enter into contracts for a combination of reasons and provided that one of the reasons is the misrepresentation this will be quite sufficient.

Types of misrepresentation

Originally misrepresentation created liability only where it was fraudulent; that is, where the person making the statement did not honestly believe that it was true. During the 19th century there was some vacillation of judicial opinion about the precise definition of fraud, which was promoted by a significantly wider definition of fraud adopted by the Court of Chancery. The narrow common law definition was applied by the House of Lords in the famous case of *Derry v. Peek* (1889)[8]. In this case a company applied for a special Act of Parliament authorising it to run trams in Plymouth. The Act passed provided that the trams might be animal powered or, if the consent of the Board of Trade were obtained, steam or mechanically powered. The directors persuaded themselves that since earlier plans had been shown to the Board of Trade without apparent objection the requirement of Board of Trade consent was a formality and issued a prospectus saying that the company had the right to use steam power. In fact the Board of Trade refused to give consent and the company was in due course wound up. The plaintiff, who had bought shares in the company, and of course suffered a loss, alleged that the directors had been fraudulent. The statement that the company was authorised to use steam power was clearly untrue but the House of Lords held that the directors were not

8-12

---

[8]   (1889) 14 App. Cas. 337.

fraudulent because they honestly believed the statement to be true. It is clear that on the facts this was a rather indulgent view since it might well have been said that the directors knew that what they said was untrue but hoped and believed that it would soon become true. However, on the basis that the directors, however foolishly and carelessly, believed their statement, the House of Lords had no difficulty in affirming that they could not be liable for fraud. To establish liability in fraud it had to be shown that the person making the statement knew that it was untrue or at least did not care whether it was true or false.

8-13   *Derry v. Peek* is still a leading decision as a definition of fraud. However, for 75 years after the decision it was treated not only as deciding that the directors were not fraudulent but that no liability at all should attach in circumstances of this kind. In fact there was an immediate statutory amendment to the decision but it was limited to the special case of share prospectuses and it was not until the decision of the House of Lords in 1963 in *Hedley Byrne v. Heller* (1964)[9] that it was established that in principle it was possible for a careless statement made by one person and relied on by another, causing that other to suffer financial loss, to give rise to liability. The precise limits of the decision in *Hedley Byrne* are still being worked out by the courts and it is clear that the statement has to be not only careless but made in circumstances in which the defendant owed a duty of care to the plaintiff. This involves consideration of such factors as whether the defendant should have contemplated that the plaintiff would have relied on him or her; and whether the plaintiff did in fact rely on the defendant, and whether in normal circumstances it was reasonable for him or her to have done so. What is clear is that there may be such a duty of care between one contracting party and another where, in the run-up to the contract, it is reasonable for that party to rely on advice which is given by the other. So in *Esso Petroleum v. Mardon* (1976)[10] the plaintiff let a filling station to the defendant on a three year lease. In the negotiations representatives of the plaintiff had expressed the opinion that the filling station might be expected to sell 200,000 gallons a year. In fact this was a careless overestimate which did not take into account the rather curious configuration of the pumps that was imposed by local planning restrictions. The defendant had no previous experience of running a filling station, though he was an experienced business man, and reasonably relied on the plaintiff's representatives who had many years' experience in the marketing of petrol. It was held that although the lease, not surprisingly, contained no mention of the forecast, the plaintiff did owe a duty of care to the defendant because it knew that the defendant

---

[9]   [1964] A.C. 465.
[10] [1976] Q.B. 801.

was relying on its expertise and the defendant was reasonable in so doing. So the defendant's counter claim to the plaintiff's action for arrears of rent, that he should recover damages for negligent misrepresentation was upheld. It should be emphasised that not every contract will give rise to liability in this way but there will be many contracts in which one party reasonably relies on the other's expertise and will have a damages action if the other party gives careless advice.

During the 1950s it increasingly became felt that the combination of the rules about terms of the contract and misrepresentation was unsatisfactory. The question was referred to the Law Reform Committee and in its tenth report in 1962 that Committee recommended a change in the law so that damages could be given for negligent misrepresentation. This proposal was made before the decision of the House of Lords in *Hedley Byrne v. Heller* and indeed implicitly assumed that the law would not be changed in the way that it was by that decision. In a rational world it would have been appropriate to reconsider the Committee's report in the light of the decision in *Hedley Byrne v. Heller* but instead the committee's report was made the basis of the Misrepresentation Act 1967.

8-14

Section 2(1) of that Act provides that:

> 'Where a person has entered into a contract after a misrepresentation has been made to him by another party thereto and as a result thereof he has suffered loss, then, if the person making the misrepresentation would be liable to damages in respect thereof had the misrepresentation been made fraudulently, that person shall be so liable notwithstanding that the misrepresentation is not made fraudulently, unless he proves that he had reasonable ground to believe and did believe up to the time the contract was made that the facts represented were true.'

The rule enacted by this sub-section significantly overlaps with the common law rule laid down in *Hedley Byrne v. Heller* but it is not the same rule. The *Hedley Byrne* rule is wider in that it applies whether or not there is a contract between plaintiff and defendant. Indeed many of the cases under *Hedley Byrne* are of this kind. On the other hand, the Misrepresentation Act only applies where the result of the misrepresentation is that a contract is entered into between the person making the representation and the person to whom it is made. However, where the Act applies it is more favourable to the plaintiff because in effect it provides for recovery of damages for negligent misrepresentation and puts on the person making the misrepresentation the burden of proving that it was not negligent. Furthermore, the statutory provision establishes liability for negligent misrepresentation in relation to all contracts, whereas the rule in *Hedley Byrne* would only apply to those contracts where one contracting party owes the other a duty of care in relation to statements made during negotiations, as in *Esso v. Mardon*.

Of course, there will remain cases in which the person making the misrepresentation is neither fraudulent nor negligent in the *Hedley Byrne* sense and can succeed in rebutting the presumption of negligence implicit in the 1967 Act. The seller in *Oscar Chess v. Williams* would be an example of such a case. Such a case may be described as one of innocent misrepresentation (though we should note that before 1963 that term was commonly applied to all cases of misrepresentation which were not fraudulent in the *Derry v. Peek* sense).

Remedies for misrepresentation

8-15   A plaintiff who has entered into a contract as a result of a misrepresentation by the defendant can recover damages either by showing that the defendant was fraudulent as in *Derry v. Peek*, or by showing that the defendant owed a duty of care and was in breach of that duty as in *Esso v. Mardon* or if the defendant is unable to show that it was not negligent in making the misrepresentation. A plaintiff, if he or she wishes, can rely on all three of these theories. In practice, prudent plaintiffs do not usually make allegations of fraud unless they have a very strong case since English courts traditionally are reluctant to stigmatise defendants as fraudulent.

The possibility of recovering damages for negligent as well as fraudulent misrepresentation substantially reduces the importance of deciding whether the statement of fact is a contractual term or a misrepresentation although it does not totally remove the significance of this distinction. It should be noted, however, that it does not follow that the same amount of damages can be recovered in a contract action as in an action for misrepresentation. The possible distinctions can perhaps best be illustrated by adopting the facts of the well known case of *Leaf v. International Galleries* (1950)[11]. In this case the plaintiff bought a painting from the defendant which the defendant incorrectly stated to have been painted by Constable. The plaintiff might have argued on these facts that it was a term of the contract that the painting was by Constable. If he could establish this the plaintiff could have recovered whatever sum of money was necessary to enable him to obtain what he should have obtained under the contract, that is a genuine Constable. On the other hand, in an action for misrepresentation, which would be substantially a tortious action, he would recover sufficient damages to enable him to be restored to his original position before the contract. If the price which was paid was a standard market price for a painting by Constable of the

---

[11]   [1950] 2 K.B. 86.

kind, the two tests would reach substantially the same result. If, however, there was a significant gap between the price paid and the open market price it would make a difference which is adopted. So in *Leaf* the plaintiff had only paid £80 for the painting and his maximum recovery in tort would therefore be £80, even assuming that the painting had actually got no value at all. On the other hand, it is likely that the open market price for the Constable, even in 1945, was several thousand pounds and in a contract action the plaintiff could expect to recover the difference between this and the value, if any, of the painting he actually received. This is of course a dramatic difference on the figures of the case. In practice it is difficult to believe that someone who buys a painting for £80 can actually believe that the other party is contracting that it is a Constable because, at least in sale by a dealer where he was contracting that the painting was by Constable, he would be asking a price at the market level of guaranteed Constables.

Alternatively, the plaintiff may seek to rescind the contract on the grounds of the defendant's misrepresentation. During the course of the 19th century it became established in the Court of Chancery that rescission was available as a general remedy to parties who had entered into contracts as a result of misrepresentation, even if the misrepresentation was entirely innocent. This is still the case. However, although rescission is a remedy easily granted where the contract has been made but not performed it can have dramatic results where the contract has been carried out because it involves unscrambling the omelette. Section 2(2) of the Misrepresentation Act 1967 has therefore conferred on the court a general power to award damages instead of allowing rescission. The right to rescission may also be lost by the operation of what are often called the bars to rescission. This again is a reflection of the fact that rescission is a potentially drastic remedy and so plaintiffs have a choice whether to rescind or not and if they choose not to rescind then they are said to affirm the contract and thereby to lose the right. There is some theoretical discussion as to whether one could lose this right simply by doing nothing. The practical answer is that plaintiffs who know they have the right to rescind are very ill-advised not to make a prompt decision. Rescission is also impossible where the plaintiff cannot restore in substance what he or she has received under the contract as the subject matter of the contract has been consumed or used, so that the Court may say that it is impossible to unscramble the omelette. Courts sometimes take a broad view on this question, particularly where the defendant is fraudulent. So if the defendant sells a business to the plaintiff on the basis of fraudulent representations as to the value of the business, the defendant may well not be able to resist rescission by arguing that the business being offered back is not the one that he or she sold. To require exact restoration in such cases would

8-16

obviously be impractical. The principle that the contract is capable of being affirmed and is not rescinded until the plaintiff chooses to do so is often expressed by saying that the contract is voidable. This means that the contract is capable of having legal effects up to the moment that it is avoided. A very important consequence of this is that rights may be conferred on third parties and that the recognition of those rights prevent rescission. Classic examples are in the case of fraudulent buyers. Suppose a buyer obtains goods from a seller by a fraudulent representation, for instance that his or her cheque is of value, and then sells the goods onto a third party before the seller discovers the fraud. This can undoubtedly create rights in the third party which cannot be defeated by rescission. This matter has already been considered in Chapter 6.

4 IMPLIED TERMS

8-17   The implied terms laid down for contracts of Sale of Goods are contained in ss. 13, 14 and 15 of the Sale of Goods Act 1979. These provisions are undoubtedly of central importance and they are amongst the most commonly quoted and relied on provisions in the whole Act. Similar provisions have been laid down by statute for contracts of hire-purchase starting with the Hire Purchase Act 1938. Much more recently general provisions applying to all contracts under which property in goods is transferred other than contracts of sale and hire-purchase have been laid down by the Supply of Goods and Services Act 1982. This Act also lays down very similar provisions in relation to contracts of hire. So we may now say that in any contract under which property or possession in goods is transferred there will be a core of basic obligations, subject only to the ability of the seller to qualify or exclude his or her liability, which will be discussed in Chapter 9.

Obligations of the seller as to description

8-18   Section 13 of the Sale of Goods Act 1979 provides:

'(a)   Where there is a contract for the sale of goods by description, there is an implied condition that the goods will correspond with the description.

(b)   If the sale is by sample as well as by description it is not sufficient that the bulk of the goods corresponds with the sample if the goods do not also correspond with the description.

(c)   A sale of goods is not prevented from being a sale by description by reason only that, being exposed for sale or hire, they are selected by the buyer.'

The first thing to note about s. 13 is that, unlike s. 14, it applies to contracts for the sale of goods of all kinds and is not limited to the case of the seller who sells goods in the course of a business. So even a private seller is bound by this section. Secondly, we should note that the section involves a paradox. If one contracts to sell a horse and delivers a cow, one might say that the cow does not fit the description of the horse contained in the contract and s. 13 applies. But one might also say that the failure to deliver a horse is a breach of an express term of the contract. This was recognised in *Andrews Brothers v. Singer* (1934)[12]. In this case the seller contracted to deliver a new Singer car under a standard printed form in which the seller sought to exclude liability for implied terms. The effectiveness of such an exclusion raises important questions which are discussed in Chapter 9. The important point for present purposes is to note that the Court of Appeal said that in any case the exclusion of implied terms was ineffective to exclude the seller's obligation to deliver a 'new Singer car' because that was an express term of the contract. The section obviously assumes that there will be cases in which a description is attached to the goods which is not an express term but becomes an implied condition by virtue of s. 13(1). This raises two central questions. The first is what is a sale by description and the second is, what words are to be treated as forming part of the description.

What is a sale by description? The Act contains no definition of a sale by description. In the 19th century it was often assumed that sales by description were to be contrasted with sales of specific goods. However, this distinction has not been maintained in the post Act law. So in *Varley v. Whipp* (1900)[13] it was held that a contract to buy a specific secondhand reaping machine which was said to have been 'new the previous year' and very little used was a sale by description. In that case, though the goods were specific, they were not present before the parties at the time that the contract was made; however in *Grant v. Australian Knitting Mills* (1936)[14] the Privy Council treated the woollen undergarments which were the subject of the action as having been sold by description, even though they were before the parties at the time of the contract. At the time of that case what is now s. 13(3) of the Act was not a part of the Act but it clearly assumes that a contract can be a sale by description despite being a contract in which the goods are specific and effectively chosen by the buyer. So in a modern supermarket most of the goods have words of description on the packaging and such contracts are clearly sales by description. The effect of this development is that virtually all contracts

---

[12]   [1934] 1 K.B. 17.
[13]   [1900] 1 Q.B. 513.
[14]   [1936] A.C. 85.

of sale are contracts for sale by description except for the very limited group of cases where the contract is not only for the sale of specific goods but no words of description are attached to the goods.

8-19   This makes the second question, *what is the description*, very important. It might be the law that if the contract is one of sale by description and words of description are used then they inevitably form part of the description. This would have dramatic practical effects. It would mean that the decision in *Oscar Chess v. Williams* was wrong because the statement that the car was a 1948 Morris should have been treated as part of the description of the car. Indeed, this was precisely the result reached in a rather similar case, *Beale v. Taylor* (1967)[15], where the seller advertised that he had a 1961 Triumph Herald for sale. In fact the car was an amalgam of two Triumph Heralds, the front and back of which had been put together. Only half of the car was of the 1961 vintage and it was held that the seller was liable because the car did not correspond with the description (the seller in this case was a private and not a commercial seller and so was not bound by s. 14 of the Act but, as noted above, was subject to s. 13).

However, it is clear that not all words which could be regarded as words of description will be treated as part of the description of the goods for the purpose of s. 13. An important case is *Ashington Piggeries v. Christopher Hill* (1972)[16]. In this case the plaintiff was in the business of compounding animal feedstuffs according to formulae provided by its customers. It was invited by the defendant to compound a vitamin fortified mink food in accordance with a formula produced by the defendant. The plaintiff made it clear that it was not expert in feeding mink but suggested substitution of herring meal for one of the ingredients in the defendant's formula. Business continued on this footing for about 12 months and the plaintiff then began to use herring meal which it bought from a supplier under a contract which stated that it was 'fair average quality of the season' and was to be taken 'with all faults and defects ... at a valuation'. In fact, unknown to any of the parties, this meal contained a chemical produced by chemical reaction which was potentially harmful to all animals and particularly to mink. These facts raised the questions of whether the plaintiff was liable to the defendant and whether the supplier was liable to the plaintiff. The House of Lords held that as between the plaintiff and defendant it was not part of the description that the goods should be suitable for feeding mink. As between the plaintiff and its supplier, the House of Lords held that the goods did comply with the description 'Norwegian herring

---

[15] [1967] 3 All E.R. 253; [1967] 1 W.L.R. 1193.
[16] [1972] A.C. 441.

meal' which was part of the description but it was not part of the description that the goods should be 'fair average quality of the season'. Of course the goods could not have been correctly described as 'meal' if there was no animal to which they could be safely fed. Why were the words 'fair average quality of the season' not part of the contractual description? The answer given by the House of Lords was that these words were not needed to identify the goods.

In *Harlingdon and Leinster Enterprises v. Christopher Hull Fine Art*   **8-20**
(1989)[17] both the defendant and the plaintiff were art dealers. In 1984 the defendant was asked to sell two oil paintings which had been described in a 1980 auction catalogue as being by Gabriele Munter, an artist of the German expressionist school. The defendant contacted the plaintiff amongst others and an employee of the plaintiff had visited the defendant's gallery. Mr Hull made it clear that he was not an expert in German expressionist paintings. The plaintiffs bought one of the paintings for £6,000 without making any more detailed enquiries about it. The invoice described the painting as being by Munter. In due course it was discovered to be a forgery. The majority of the Court of Appeal held that it was not part of the description of the painting that it was by Munter. The principal test relied on by the Court of Appeal was that of reliance. It was pointed out that paintings are often sold accompanied by views as to their provenance. These statements may run the whole gamut of possibilities from a binding undertaking that the painting is by a particular artist to statements that the painting is in a particular style. Successful artists are of course often copied by contemporaries, associates and pupils. It would be odd if the legal effect of every statement about the identity of the artist was treated in the same way. This is certainly not how business is done since much higher prices are paid where the seller is guaranteeing the attribution and the Court of Appeal therefore argued that it makes much better sense to ask whether the buyer has relied on the seller's statement before deciding to treat the statement as a part of the description. On any view this case is very close to the line. It appears plausibly arguable that the majority did not give enough weight to the wording of the invoice or to the fact that the buyers appear to have paid a 'warranted Munter' price. It should be noted that the buyers did not argue, as they might have done, that it was an express term of the contract that the painting was by Munter.

In this last case, the Court of Appeal held that as the attribution to   **8-21**
Munter was the only piece of potentially descriptive labelling attached to the painting it was not a sale by description. In other cases, such as the *Ashington Piggeries* case, it would be clear that some of the words

---

[17] [1991] 1 Q.B. 564; [1990] 1 All E.R. 737.

attached are words of description but it may be held that other words are not. Whether one is asking the question as to whether there is a sale by description or the question what is a description, the question whether the words are used to identify the goods and are relied on by the buyer will be highly relevant factors.

Where there has been a sale by description, the court then has to decide whether or not the goods correspond with the description. In a number of cases, courts have taken very strict views on this question. An extreme example is *Re Moore and Landauer* (1921)[18]. That was a contract for the purchase of Australian canned fruit. It was stated that the cans were in cases containing 30 tins each. The seller delivered the right number of cans but in cases which contained only 24 tins. It was not suggested that there was anything wrong with the fruit or that it made any significant difference whether the fruit was in cases of 30 or 24 cans. Nevertheless, it was held that the goods delivered did not correspond with the contract description. Similarly, in *Arcos v. Ronaasen* (1933)[19] the contract was for a quantity of staves half an inch thick. In fact, only some 5% of the staves delivered were half an inch thick, though nearly all were less than 9/16th of an inch thick. The evidence was that the staves were perfectly satisfactory for the purpose for which the buyer had bought them - that is, the making of cement barrels - but the House of Lords held that the goods did not correspond with the description. The buyer is unlikely to take a point of this kind unless he or she is anxious to escape from the contract, for example because the price of tinned food or wooden staves has fallen and it is possible to buy more cheaply on the market elsewhere. It may be thought that some of these decisions lean somewhat too much to the side of the buyer. In *Reardon Smith v. Hansen-Tangen* (1976)[20], Lord Wilberforce said that these decisions were excessively technical. In that case, there were a series of transactions to charter and sub-charter a ship, as yet unbuilt, the size and dimensions of the ship were set out in the contract and the ship was described as 'motor tank vessel called yard number 354 Osaka Zosen'. The ship which was tendered when built complied with the technical specification but had been built at a different yard and therefore had the yard number Oshima 004. The tanker market having collapsed, the charterers sought to escape by saying that the ship did not comply with the description. The House of Lords rejected this argument. The technical reason for doing so was that the yard number did not form part of the description but in reaching this conclusion the House of Lords were clearly influenced by the underlying commercial realities of this situation.

---

[18] [1921] 2 K.B. 519.
[19] [1933] A.C. 470.
[20] [1976] 1 W.L.R. 989; [1976] 3 All E.R. 570.

Merchantable quality

Section 14 of the Sale of Goods Act 1979 provides:

'(1)   Except as provided by this section and s. 15 below and subject to any other enactment, there is no implied condition or warranty about the quality of fitness for any particular purpose of goods supplied under a contract of sale.

(2)   Where the seller sells goods in the course of a business, there is an implied condition that the goods supplied under the contract are of merchantable quality, except that there is no such condition -

> (a) as regards defects specifically drawn to the buyer's attention before the contract is made; or

> (b) if the buyer examines the goods before the contract is made, as regards defects which that examination ought to reveal.

(6)   Goods of any kind are of merchantable quality within the meaning of sub-section (2) above if they are as fit for the purpose or purposes for which goods of that kind are commonly bought as it is reasonable to expect having regard to any description applied to them, the price (if relevant) and all the other relevant circumstances.'

The obligations stated in these sub-sections, as in the parallel obligation as to fitness for purpose set out in s. 14(3), apply only to a seller who sells goods in the course of a business. Section 61(1) says that 'business' includes a profession and the activities of any government department (including a Northern Ireland department) or local or public authority. This is obviously not a definition of business but an extension of it to include activities by bodies which would not fall within the natural meaning of the word business. It should be noted that the Act does not say that the seller must be in the business of selling goods of that kind and indeed members of professions or central or local government will not normally be in the business of selling goods of a particular kind but may be within the scope of s. 14. This reflects a change from the original 1893 version of the section under which the implied obligation as to merchantable quality only applied where the goods were 'bought by description from a seller who deals in goods of that description'. It is clear that the disappearance of these words means a significant widening of the scope of the section. There will be relatively few cases which are outside it except that of the private seller who is, for instance, disposing of his or her car. Even a private seller maybe caught where he or she employs a business to sell on his or her behalf because of the provisions of s. 14(5) which provides:

'The preceding provisions of this section apply to a sale by a person who in the course of a business is acting as agent for another as they apply to a sale by a principal in the course of a business, except where that other is not selling in the course of a business and either the buyer knows that fact or reasonable steps are taken to bring it to the notice of the buyer before the contract is made.'

This sub-section was considered by the House of Lords in *Boyer v Thomson* [1995][21]. In this case a private seller instructed a business to sell a cabin cruiser on his behalf. The buyer purchased the boat thinking that it was being sold by the business and that it was owned by the business. It was agreed that the boat was not of merchantable quality. The buyer did not know that the owner of the cabin cruiser was a private person and no reasonable steps had been taken to bring that to the buyer's notice. The House of Lords held that the effect of s. 14(5) was, in the circumstances, that both the principal and the agent were liable to the buyer.

8-23   It will be noted that the obligation that the goods shall be of merchantable quality applies to 'goods supplied under the contract' and not to the goods which are sold. Obviously the goods which are sold would usually be the goods which are supplied under the contract but this will not always be the case. A good example is *Wilson v. Rickett Cockerell* (1954)[22] where there was a contract for the sale of Coalite. A consignment of Coalite was delivered but included a piece of explosive which had been accidentally mixed with the Coalite and which exploded when put on the fire. This case was decided under the 1893 version of the Act which did not expressly have the reference to 'goods supplied under the contract' but the Court of Appeal held that the obligation that the goods should be of merchantable quality applied to all the goods which were supplied under the contract and of course it followed that the delivery was defective. The amendment of the wording in the present version of the Act clearly confirms the correctness of this decision.

The expression 'merchantable quality' is not one which is in modern popular usage even amongst merchants. What does it mean? The 1893 Act did not contain any definition of the expression. The present version of the Act contains the definition contained in s. 14(6). In *Rogers v. Parish* (1987)[23] the Court of Appeal said that there was no need to go back to cases before 1973 when the definition was first introduced. This is no doubt correct as far as presentation of cases in court is concerned but the cases between 1893 and 1973 are useful as

---

[21]   [1995] 3 All E.R. 125.

[22]   [1954] 1 Q.B. 598.

[23]   [1987] 2 W.L.R. 353.

illustrating the sort of problems which arise. It is thought that the definition in s. 14(6) is intended to encapsulate the reasoning in most of the previous cases and to resolve some unclear points rather than to reverse any major earlier decision.

A reasonable translation of the words 'merchantable quality' would mean 'commercially saleable', that is that the goods are in a condition in which a commercial seller could sell them and find a buyer. Since the goods are in fact the subject of a contract of sale in order for there to be a dispute, it is clear that the seller will have sold them and that they are, in a sense, saleable. Obviously, this cannot be the point however. The critical question is whether the goods would be saleable if the buyer knew of the qualities which they in fact possessed. Clearly this raises a series of questions depending upon what is 'wrong' with the goods. No doubt there are some goods which are so defective that nobody would buy them whatever the price. In many cases, however, goods could be sold if the price reflected what was wrong with them or could be sold to some buyers who wanted them for other purposes. In some cases, whether a buyer would buy goods knowing their condition depends upon the price. So in *B S Brown v. Craiks* (1970)[24] the buyer ordered a quantity of cloth which was to be used for making dresses. The cloth delivered was unsuitable for making dresses though it would have been suitable for industrial purposes. The buyer had not told the seller for what purpose the cloth was required. The contract price was 36.25d per yard which was higher, but not much higher, than the going rate for industrial cloth. The House of Lords held that the goods were of merchantable quality. The buyer had paid a high price in the industrial range but had not paid a 'dress price'. If the facts had been exactly the same except that the price had been 50d per yard the result would presumably have been different, since in such a case there would have been an irresistible argument that the seller was charging a dress price and therefore had to supply goods of dress quality.

In other cases it will be very important under what description the goods are sold. In *Kendall v. Lillico* (1969)[25] the plaintiffs bought animal feeding stuff for pheasants which was contaminated with a substance which was contained in Brazilian ground nut extraction which was one of the ingredients which made up the feeding stuff. The defendant settled the claim of the plaintiffs and claimed over against the suppliers. Although the suppliers had supplied Brazilian ground nut extraction which was contaminated, they were not supplying goods of unmerchantable quality because the Brazilian ground nut extraction was

8-24

8-25

---

24 [1970] 1 All E.R. 823; [1970] 1 W.L.R. 752.
25 [1969] 2 A.C. 31.

perfectly suitable as a basis for feeding stuff for poultry. The purpose for which the goods bought are to be used is of critical importance in relation to s. 14(3) as we shall see below. It is also important, however, as to s. 14(2). If the extraction had been sold as poultry feed, it would not have been merchantable because feed which is poisonous to poultry cannot be sold as poultry feed. If sold as animal food, it would be a completely different matter since the extraction was perfectly suitable for feeding to many, though not to all, animals. This illustrates a very important general proposition, which is that if the goods have a number of potential purposes, they will usually be of merchantable quality if they can be used for one of the purposes for which such goods are commonly used, unless they are sold under a contract description which points to a single purpose for which they cannot effectively be used. The difference in this respect between *B S Brown v. Craiks* and *Kendall v. Lillico* is that in *Brown* there were two purposes, one of which commanded a higher price than the other, whereas in *Kendall* the various purposes appear to have commanded much the same price.

8-26

It would appear that the decisions discussed above would be the same under the 1979 statutory definition. In *Aswan Engineering v. Lupdine* (1987)[26], the Court of Appeal rejected an argument that the wording of s. 14(6) meant that the goods were not of merchantable quality unless they were fit for all the purposes for which goods of that kind were commonly bought.

There has been considerable discussion about the relationship between the requirement of merchantable quality and the realities of buying new cars. It is extremely probable that a new car will have some defects. Normally the buyer will in fact expect to get these defects put right under the manufacturer's warranty. Does this affect the seller's obligation to deliver a car of merchantable quality? It appears not. In *Bernstein v. Pamson Motors* (1987)[27] the plaintiff bought a new car and some three weeks later when it had done only 140 miles, it broke down because the engine completely seized up. It was held that this made the car unmerchantable. Similarly in *Rogers v. Parish* a new Range Rover had, during its first six months of life, a whole series of defects as to the engine, gear box, body and oil seals. The defects did not make the car unsafe or unroadworthy and each of them was put right but the Court of Appeal held that there was a breach of the requirement of merchantable quality. The Court of Appeal thought that the manufacturer's obligations under the guarantee were irrelevant to the legal position of

---

[26] [1987] 1 All E.R. 135; [1987] 1 W.L.R. 1.
[27] [1987] 2 All E.R. 220.

buyer and seller. Any argument that the buyer must expect some defects in a new car could hardly apply on the facts of either of these cases because no buyer would expect his or her car to seize up after 140 miles or to require a replacement engine or gear box in the first six months of its life. These principles are equally applicable in principle to secondhand cars (or indeed other secondhand goods), though obviously the reasonable expectations of a buyer of secondhand goods will not be identical with the reasonable expectations of the buyer of new goods.

In *Shine v. General Guarantee Corporation* (1988)[28] the subject of the sale was a 1981 Fiat X1-9 sports car which was offered for sale secondhand in August 1982 at £4,595. The evidence was that this was the going rate for such a car in good condition. In fact, for some 24 hours in January 1982, the car had been totally submerged in water and had been written off by the insurance company. The Court of Appeal held that the car was not of merchantable quality since no-one would have bought the car knowing of its condition without at least a substantial reduction of the price. It will be seen that this reason in effect, in a case of this kind, requires the seller either to lower the price or to draw the buyer's attention to the relevant defect.

8-27

It will be noted that the obligation in s. 14(2) of the Sale of Goods Act 1979 is excluded either as regards a defect which is specifically drawn to the buyer's attention before the contract is made or, where the buyer examines the goods before the contract is made, to defects which that examination ought to have revealed. The latter proviso requires a further word of comment. Of course, examination does not exclude liability for defects which would not have been revealed by careful examination. Many of the defects discussed in this chapter are of this kind. Furthermore, this section does not require the buyer to examine the goods so he or she is not prevented from complaining when he or she does not examine at all the defects which a reasonable examination would have revealed. The practical effect of this is that the buyer ought either to carry out a careful examination or no examination at all. To carry out a cursory examination is likely to produce the worst of both worlds.

The Sale and Supply of Goods Act 1994 substitutes a new s. 14(2) for the existing s. 14(2) of the Act. The 1979 and 1994 versions of s. 14(2) are set out below:

'SALE OF GOODS ACT 1979	SALE AND SUPPLY OF GOODS ACT 1994
14 Implied terms about quality or fitness	14 Implied terms about quality or fitness
(2) Where the seller sells goods in the course of a business, there is an implied condition that the goods	(2) Where the seller sells goods in the course of a business, there is an implied <u>term</u> that the goods

---

28   [1988] 1 All E.R. 911.

supplied under the contract are of merchantable quality, except that there is no such condition -

(a) as regards defects specifically drawn to the buyer's attention before the contract is made; or

(b) if the buyer examines the goods before the contract is made, as regards defects which that examination ought to reveal.

supplied under the contract are of satisfactory quality. merchantable quality, except that there is no such condition -

(A) For the purposes of this Act, goods are of satisfactory quality if they meet the standard that a reasonable person would regard as satisfactory, taking account of any description of the goods, the price (if relevant) and all the other relevant circumstances. as regards defects specifically drawn to the buyer's attention before the contract is made; or

(B) For the purposes of this Act, the quality of goods includes their state and condition and the following (among others) are in appropriate cases aspects of the quality of goods – if the buyer examines the goods before the contract is made, as regards defects which that examination ought to reveal.

(a) fitness for all the purposes for which goods of the kind in question are commonly supplied.

(b) appearance and finish.

(c) freedom from minor defects.

(d) safety, and

(e) durability.

(C) The term implied by subsection (2) above does not extend to any matter making the quality of goods unsatisfactory –

(a) which is specifically drawn to the buyer's attention before the contract is made.

(b) where the buyer examines the goods before the contract is made, which that examination ought to reveal, or

(c) <u>in the case of a contract for sale by sample, which would have been apparent on a reasonable examination of the sample'.</u>

[New words in the 1994 version are underlined. Deletions are indicated by striking through.]

The new version makes a number of changes. Perhaps the most obvious is the replacement of the words 'merchantable quality' by the words 'satisfactory quality'. The thinking behind this change was that the expression 'merchantable quality' is not used anywhere, either in English law or in colloquial English, except in the context of the Sale of Goods Act. It is, therefore, an expression which is understood only by lawyers specialising in sale of goods law. It was thought that buyers and sellers who were told that the goods must be of merchantable quality would not get much guidance from this statement. This may be agreed, but the problem was to find an appropriate substitute. The Act is based on a Law Commission Report of 1987 in which it had been suggested that 'merchantable quality' should become 'acceptable quality'. It may perhaps be thought to matter relatively little which of these words is used. Although 'acceptable' and 'satisfactory' are both words which are used every day and which most people will understand, they do not by themselves help buyers and sellers to know at all clearly where the line is to be drawn between acceptable and unacceptable and satisfactory and unsatisfactory goods. So, this change by itself is really almost entirely cosmetic.

Some of the textual changes in the 1994 version are simply rearrangements of provisions which appear in the 1979 version. So, the exceptions from a liability to deliver goods of a satisfactory quality where the defect is specifically drawn to the buyer's attention or the buyer has examined the goods and that examination ought to have revealed the actual defects which are contained in s. 14(2)(a) and (b) are now to be found in s. 14(2)(C)(a) and (b). The substantial changes relate to the definition of 'satisfactory quality'.

Part of the definition in s. 14(6) of the 1979 Act now appears in s. 14(2)(A), that is the reference to 'taking account of any description of the goods, the price (if relevant) and all the other relevant circumstances'. One change relates to the wording of that part of s. 14(6) which refers to goods being 'as fit for the purpose or purposes for which goods of that kind are commonly bought as it is reasonable to expect'. The decision in *Aswan Engineering v. Lupdine* that goods were of merchantable quality within this definition if they were fit for any one of the purposes for which they were commonly bought has in effect been reversed by the present provision contained in s. 14(2)(B)(a) which means that goods will not be of satisfactory quality unless they are fit for all the purposes for which such goods are commonly supplied. This might appear a rather technical change but, in fact, it is of considerable practical importance. It substantially reduces the need to rely on s. 14(3) and show that the seller knows the buyer's purpose in buying the goods. Where goods are bought for one of a number of common purposes, the buyer will be able to rely on s. 14(2) if they are not fit for all those purposes even, it would appear, if they are fit for the purpose for which the buyer requires them. Of course, if they are fit for the purpose for which the buyer actually requires them, the buyer will usually suffer no loss but it is likely that, sooner or later, a case will occur where the buyer tries to get out of the contract because of some movement in the market and uses this as an excuse. Suppose, for instance, that the buyer is a dairy farmer who buys the goods for the purposes of feeding to cows and that the same material is commonly fed to pigs but that the particular batch, though perfectly suitable for feeding cows, will not do for pigs. It would appear that if the buyer realises this at the time of delivery, he could probably reject under the present wording.

The other changes which are made are contained in s. 14(2)(B)(c), (d) and (e). These add further detail to the definition of merchantable/satisfactory quality. There were very few reported cases which involved consideration of whether these issues fell within the statutory definition as to quality. It was said that there are a large number of small cases coming before county courts or the arbitration process in small claims courts where different judges were taking different views as to where to draw the line. This is obviously a matter of particular importance to consumers. Is a consumer who buys a new washing machine and finds it has a major scratch across the paint-work bound to accept it; is a consumer whose washing machine stops and is unrepairable after 13 months' use entitled to complain that he expected to get three to five years' repairable use out of the washing machine? Is a combination of minor defects on your new motor car sufficient to make it unsatisfactory? The wording of the new section must make an affirmative answer to these questions much more likely.

8-28　　**Fitness for purpose**

Section 14(3) of the Sale of Goods Act 1979 provides:

'Where the seller sells goods in the course of a business and the buyer, expressly or by implication, makes known -

(a)   to the seller, or

(b)   where the purchase price or part of it is payable by instalments and the goods were previously sold by a credit-broker to the seller, to that credit-broker, any particular purpose for which the goods are being bought, there is an implied condition that the goods supplied under the contract are reasonably fit for that purpose, whether or not that is a purpose for which such goods are commonly supplied, except where the circumstances show that the buyer does not rely, or that it is unreasonable for him to rely, on the skill or judgment of the seller or credit-broker.'

It should perhaps be noted that in the 1893 version of the Act the implied term about fitness for purpose was s. 14(1) and the implied term about merchantable quality was s. 14(2). This change in the order may reflect a change in view as to which of the obligations is primary and which is secondary. It should be emphasised that in practice, buyers who complain of the goods being defective very commonly rely on both merchantable quality and fitness for purpose arguments and that there is a significant degree of overlap. Indeed, the buyer may rely also on arguments about description and again there will be overlap between s. 13 and s. 14(2) because whether the goods are of merchantable quality will often turn on the description under which they are sold. The two major differences between s. 14(2) and s. 14(3) are that where goods are sold for a number of purposes, the buyer may have a better chance of succeeding under s. 14(3) if he or she has disclosed the particular purpose for which he or she requires the goods to the seller; on the other hand, to establish liability under s. 14(3) the buyer has to show that he or she has relied on the skill and judgment of the seller. In many cases this may easily be inferred but there is no such requirement at all in relation to the obligation of merchantable quality under s. 14(2). A layman reading s. 14(3) for the first time might be forgiven for thinking that in order to be able to rely on it the buyer must do something to draw to the seller's attention the purpose for which he or she requires the goods. However, this is not the way in which the section has been construed. Where goods are produced for a single purpose, the court will easily infer that the goods are being bought for that purpose even though all that the buyer does is to ask for goods of that kind. So it has been held that to buy beer or milk makes it clear that one is buying it for drinking; that to buy tinned salmon makes it clear that it has been bought for the purpose of being eaten; that to buy a hot water bottle makes it clear that it has been bought for the purpose of being filled with very hot water and put in a bed and to buy a catapult makes it clear that it has been bought for the purpose of catapulting stones. In other words, if there is a single purpose, it is easy to infer that goods must be fit for that purpose and if the seller is a seller of goods of that kind it is easy to infer that the buyer is relying on the seller's skill and judgment.

8-29   It should be emphasised that liability under this sub-section, as indeed under s. 14(2), turns on the goods not being of merchantable quality or fitness for purpose respectively. It is no defence for the seller to show that he or she did all that could possibly have been done to ensure that the goods were fit for the purpose or of merchantable quality if he or she has failed to do so.

The position is different where goods have more than one purpose. We may distinguish at least two variants on this possibility. One is where goods are used for a purpose which is a specialised and more demanding version of the standard purpose. Suppose that a buyer is buying pig food to feed to a herd of pigs which have super-sensitive stomachs. Suppose further that he or she orders a pig food from a supplier who supplies pig food which would be entirely suitable for pigs with normally robust digestions. In that case if that is all that has happened the supplier will not be in breach of contract since although what has happened has revealed the ordinary purpose for which the goods were required, it does not reveal the extraordinary requirements of the buyer. In order to be able to complain that the pig food was not suitable for the pigs, the buyer would need to make it clear to the supplier more precisely what his or her requirements were.

Alternatively the goods may be capable of being used for a range of purposes which are different. For instance, as in *Kendall v. Lillico* where the goods were suitable for feeding cattle but not suitable for feeding poultry. A buyer could recover on these facts if, but only if, he or she made it clear to the seller that the purpose was to buy food for feeding poultry. In fact, in that case, it was held that the seller did have a sufficient knowledge of the buyer's purpose to make him liable and this case is therefore a good example of goods which were merchantable because they were commercially saleable as cattle feed but which were not fit for the buyer's purpose. Similarly, in *Ashington Piggeries v. Christopher Hill* the goods did comply with the contract description so that there was no liability under s. 13 but it was held that the buyer had adequately disclosed to the seller his intention to feed the compound to mink and therefore to found liability on s. 14(3).

8-30   Sales by sample

Section 15 of the Sale of Goods Act 1979 provides:

'(1)   A contract of sale is a contract for sale by sample where there is an express or implied term to that effect in the contract.

(2)   In the case of a contract for sale by sample there is an implied condition -

(a) that the bulk will correspond with the sample in quality;

(b) that the buyer will have a reasonable opportunity of comparing the bulk with the sample;

(c) that the goods will be free from any defect, <u>rendering them unmerchantable</u>[29], which would not be apparent on reasonable examination of the sample.

(3)   In sub-section (2)(c) above 'unmerchantable' is to be construed in accordance with section 14(6) above.'

The Act contains no definition of what is a sale by sample other than the wholly unhelpful statement in s. 15(1) which leaves quite in the air the question where there is an implied term that the sale is by sample. It is easy enough to see what is the central transaction to which this section applies. Sales by sample are common in the sale of bulk commodities because a seller can display to the buyer a sample of what he or she has and the buyer can agree that he or she will take so many pounds or tons. The sample here in effect largely replaces the need for any description by words of the goods and it is therefore natural to imply, as in s. 15(2)(a), a term that the bulk will correspond with the sample in quality.

However, there are other transactions of a quite different kind which could be regarded as sales by sample. So, for instance, a fleet manager of a large company may be deciding what car to buy for the company's representatives. He or she might very well be shown an example of a particular car and as a result place an order for 200. Would it follow that the 200 cars should be identical in quality with the one which he or she was shown?

Other implied terms

The terms set out in ss. 13, 14 and 15 of the Sale of Goods Act 1979 **8-31** are the basic implied terms which will be incorporated into every contract of sale subject to the possibility of the seller successfully seeking to exclude them in the contract. However, there is nothing in the Act to say that this list is complete. In principle, there seems to be no reason why the general principles about implication of terms in the general law of contract should not apply. So, if a contract of sale is made against a background of a particular trade or local custom, it will be open for one party to seek to show that the custom exists, is reasonable and contracts of sale made in this particular context are regarded by those in the trade or living in the locality as subject to this implied term.

---

[29] The underlined words are replaced by 'making their quality unsatisfactory' by the Sale and Supply of Goods Act 1994.

Similarly, there is no reason why a party should not seek to show that in a particular contract a term is to be implied in order to give business efficacy to the contract. Perhaps the best example of an implied term which is not explicitly set out in the Act but which has been recognised is shown in *Mash & Murrell v. Joseph I Emmanuel* (1961)[30]. In this case there was a contract for the sale of Cyprus potatoes cif Liverpool. On arrival in Liverpool the potatoes were found to be uneatable but the evidence was that they were eatable on loading in Limassol. Diplock J said that liability turned on the reason why the potatoes were uneatable. There were various possible reasons such as bad stowage or inadequate ventilation during the voyage. These would not have been the seller's fault and the risk of these possibilities would pass to the buyer on shipment, leaving the buyer to an action against the carrier. However, one possibility was that the potatoes, although eatable when shipped, were not in a fit state to withstand a normal voyage from Cyprus to Liverpool. Diplock J said that it was an implied term of the contract in the circumstances that the goods would be fit to withstand an ordinary journey. The Court of Appeal differed with the conclusion that Diplock J reached but not with his analysis of this point.

Rights and remedies

8-32   The Law Commission produced a consultative document in 1983 and a full report in 1987. The report shows that there is a tension between the definition of the seller's obligations which we have just discussed and the buyer's remedies for breach of those obligations which is discussed in Chapter 10. Under the existing framework of the Sale of Goods Act, each of the implied obligations in ss. 13, 14 and 15 is said to be a condition and, as will be explained in Chapter 10, this is taken to mean that if there is any breach of the obligation the buyer is entitled to reject the goods. Courts have sometimes thought that although the goods were defective, the defects were not of a kind which ought to have entitled the buyer to reject the goods. The leading example of this is *Cehave v. Bremer* (1976)[31]. That was a contract for the sale of citrus pulp pellets which were intended by the buyer to be used for animal feed. There was damage to the goods and the buyer purported to reject them. There was then a forced sale by the Admiralty Court in Holland at which the buyer rebought the goods at a much lower price and used them for feeding cattle. In these circumstances, the Court of Appeal was looking for a good reason to find that the buyer was not entitled to reject. What it did was to hold that the defect in the goods did

---

[30]   [1961] 1 All E.R. 485; [1962] 1 All E.R. 77.
[31]   [1976] Q.B. 44.

not make them unmerchantable though it clearly reduced somewhat their value. The problem with this approach is that although it may be perfectly reasonable to restrict the buyer's right to reject the goods, it does not usually follow from this that the buyer should be left without any remedy at all. Often the buyer ought to have a remedy at least in money terms to reflect the difference in value between what he or she contracted for and what he or she has received. There is also an important difference as far as rejection is concerned between consumers and those who buy goods commercially, particularly those who buy goods for resale. It is often perfectly reasonable to say to such buyers that they ought to put up with the goods and be satisfied with a reduction in price; it is much less commonly reasonable to say this to a consumer. This perception underlies further changes made by the Sale and Supply of Goods Act 1994 which are discussed in Chapter 10.

5   LIABILITY IN TORT

This book is primarily concerned with liability in contract between   **8-33**
buyer and seller but completeness requires some mention of claims which the buyer may have against other people, especially the manufacturer. In some circumstances the buyer may have a contract claim against the manufacturer. Sometimes indeed the manufacturer and seller are the same person and in that case, of course, no problem arises. In other cases, although the manufacturer and seller are not the same person, the manufacturer may have entered into a separate contract with the buyer. The most obvious way in which such a contract might come about is by the operation of the manufacturer's guarantee. Most consumer durables are now issued accompanied by a guarantee in which the manufacturer typically promises to repair or replace the goods if they do not work within a period, generally a year.

Curiously enough, there is surprisingly little authority in English law as to whether manufacturers' guarantees give rise to a contract between manufacturer and customer. The leading case is the classic one of *Carlill v. Carbolic Smokeball Co.* (1893)[32]. In this case the plaintiff, Mrs Carlill, bought a smokeball manufactured by the defendant from a retail chemist, relying on elaborate advertising by the defendant in which it offered to pay £100 to anyone who used the smokeball according to the directions and then caught flu. This is a rather special case because the claims made by the manufacturer were very explicit and specific. Typically modern manufacturers' advertising tends to be couched in much less contractual language. The technical problem with giving

---

[32]   [1893] 1 Q.B. 256.

contractual force to the manufacturer's guarantee is that often the customer will not know of the guarantee until after he or she has bought the goods and further he or she will often not have done anything in exchange for the guarantee. So there may be difficulty in satisfying the technical requirement of the English law of contract that promises are only binding if they are supported by consideration. On the other hand, it is reasonable to assume that a reputable manufacturer would be very reluctant to go back on the guarantee because of the very bad adverse publicity which would be attracted. This no doubt accounts for the absence of reported cases on the subject. Nevertheless, the situation is not wholly satisfactory especially as many guarantees are couched in somewhat evasive language or impose onerous restrictions such as that the goods should be returned in the original packaging if they fail to work. The practice of consumer guarantees was the subject of a report issued by the Director General of Fair Trading in June 1986, urging higher standards on those who issue guarantees and hinting at the possibility of legislation in the long run.

8-34   Of course, the manufacturer will often be liable in contract to the person to whom it has supplied the goods and the buyer may therefore be able to start off a chain of actions in which the buyer sues the retailer, the retailer sues the wholesaler and the wholesaler sues the manufacturer. By this means, if the fault in the goods is due to the manufacturer, liability can often be shunted back to it by a series of actions. However, this would not always be possible. The manufacturer may in fact be outside the country and difficult to sue; someone may have successfully sold the goods subject to an exclusion or limitation clause which prevents liability being passed up the chain or it may be that the chain breaks down in some other way. For instance, in *Lambert v. Lewis* (1982)[33] the buyer complained of a defective towing hook which had been fitted to his Land Rover. The buyer knew who had fitted the towing hook and it was clear who the manufacturer was but the garage which had supplied the towing hook did not know from which of a number of possible wholesalers it had bought the towing hook. In these circumstances, the garage which had supplied the towing hook could not pass liability on because it could not identify the other party to the contract and it was not allowed to jump over this chasm and sue the manufacturer direct.

The question arises whether the buyer can sue the manufacturer direct in tort. Before 1932 it was widely believed that the answer to this question was no and that the only actions in respect of defective goods were contractual actions. This was clearly revealed to be wrong by the

---

[33] [1982] A.C. 225.

majority decision of the House of Lords in *Donoghue v. Stevenson* (1932)[34]. In this case, two ladies entered a café in Paisley and one bought for both of them ice cream and ginger beer. When the second lady poured part of the ginger beer on her ice cream, a snail came out of the bottle. On these facts, the plaintiff had no contract with anyone because she had not bought the ginger beer and of course her friend was not liable in contract since she had given it to her. The majority of the House of Lords held that on such facts the plaintiff could sue the manufacturer on the basis that the manufacturer owed her a duty of care to prepare the product with reasonable care; that a reasonably careful manufacturer of ginger beer would not allow snails to get into the bottle; that since the bottle was opaque there was no reasonable possibility of intermediate examination which might detect the snail before it reached the plaintiff and that the plaintiff reasonably foreseeably suffered physical injury as a result. It has never since been seriously doubted that this decision is correct and many decisions have followed and built upon it.

Although it is common to talk of liability in terms of manufacturers, liability in fact rests upon any person who produces or handles goods in circumstances where it is reasonably foreseeable that carelessness in the handling of the goods will cause physical injury or property damage and there is in fact carelessness. So in appropriate cases liability can attach to wholesalers, repairers, those who service goods and indeed on sellers. So, for instance, a seller of a motor car would normally do a detailed check on the car before delivering it in order to discover defects. The seller who failed to do this would be liable in tort not only to the buyer (who has in any case an action in contract) but to anyone else foreseeably injured, for example a member of the buyer's family (who would, of course, have no contract action).

The defendant will not be liable in such an action unless he or she **8-35** can be shown to have been negligent. This is a fundamental difference between tort actions and contract actions which do not require any proof of negligence. In a case such as *Donoghue v. Stevenson* the requirement to prove negligence was not a serious limitation on the plaintiff's chances of success, since in practice a court is likely, very easily, to infer that careful bottling should exclude the possibility of snails getting into the bottle. In practice, the manufacturer in such a case has to lead evidence of his or her system and is likely to be impaled on one limb or other of a dilemma. Either he or she shows that the system is usually foolproof, in which case it is likely to be inferred that it must have broken down in the particular case, or he or she shows the system is vulnerable in which case he or she is negligent for not having a foolproof system. Malfunctions in the production system of this kind are reasonably easy

---

[34]   [1932] A.C. 562.

for plaintiffs to contend with. Plaintiffs have much more difficulty when they wish to argue that all specimens of a particular product are defective. This was the problem which confronted the victims of the drug thalidomide who had to try to show that not only was the drug harmful to foetuses but that the manufacturers and distributors were negligent not to have realised this. In practice, in a contested action, a plaintiff has very serious difficulty in doing this. It is this, amongst other things, which has led to the introduction of a regime of product liability (see below).

There is another major limit on liability in tort. As the law is currently understood, it seems that plaintiffs can only recover where they have suffered either physical injury or property damage. So, if a manufacturer of a motor car negligently installs a braking system and the plaintiff has an accident and is injured, the plaintiff should be able to recover but if the plaintiff discovers that the braking system is defective and stops driving the car before having an accident, he or she will not be able to recover in tort against the manufacturer for the loss of value of the car because it is not as good a car as it was thought to be. To put it another way, actions for shoddy goods lie in contract and not in tort.

8-36   The difficulty of proving negligence in certain types of defective product have led to calls for the adoption of a regime in which the liability of the manufacturer should be strict, that is, should depend solely on the establishment that the goods were defective and not on a requirement to prove that the manufacturer was at fault. Such a system has been adopted in the United States by judicial development but it has always been assumed that in this country the change would require legislation. Both the Law Commission (in 1977) and the Royal Commission on Civil Liberty and Compensation for Death or Personal Injury, usually called the Pearson Commission (in March 1978) recommended statutory change to introduce such a regime. It appeared that this advice had fallen on deaf ears until in July 1985 the European Community adopted a product liability directive, Parliament enacted Part I of the Consumer Protection Act 1987 which from 1 March 1988 introduced a product liability regime into English law. This Act does not remove any of the existing remedies which somebody damaged by defective goods may have. What is does is to introduce an additional set of remedies. In practice, it is likely that plaintiffs injured by defective goods after 1 March 1988 will seek to argue for liability both in contract or tort under the old law and under the Consumer Protection Act. Although where the Act applies plaintiffs would usually be better off suing under the Act than in an action in tort, they would often still be better off pursuing a contract action, if they have one.

8-37   To give a detailed account of the Act would be out of place here but some mention should be made of the main features. The primary thrust of the Act is to increase the possibility of an effective remedy for someone who suffers personal injury or death. There is, however, a subsidiary right in respect of damage to the property of individuals (though not of companies) subject to a minimum of £275. Liability attaches to the producer, who would in most cases be the manufacturer, but there are certain situations where someone else is treated as the producer. So, if the goods are manufactured outside the European Community the first person to import them into the Community is treated as the producer. This is so as to ensure that there is an effective defendant within the Community. Similarly, if people hold themselves out as the producer by putting their own name on the goods, as in the case of own brand goods sold by supermarkets, they become the producer, as may someone who having supplied the goods, fails to comply with a request from someone injured by the goods to identify either the producer or the importer.

Liability relates to defective products but a defective product is defined in terms of safety. A product is defective if it is not as safe as 'persons generally are entitled to expect'. For the purpose of assessing this, a court is required to take into account all the relevant circumstances and, in particular:

'(a) the manner and purposes for which the product has been marketed and any instructions or warnings which accompany it;

(b) what might reasonably be expected to be done with or in relation to the product; and

(c) the time when the product was supplied by its producer to another.'

So the court needs to consider both the purposes for which the goods are put into circulation and also the ways in which they might be used. Many of the leading cases in the United States have involved misuse of the product by the consumer and it is thought that a prudent producer should anticipate likely forms of misuse, though no doubt there are some forms of misuse so gross that the manufacturer should not be expected to guard against them. The form in which instructions for the use of the product is given will be very important. The manufacturer needs to give thought not only to the content of the instructions but also to practical ways of keeping the instructions in a way which is effectively close to the product. In many cases, instructions are put in booklets which are put in drawers and lost or in cardboard slips which were attached to a product when bought but soon become detached. So, for instance, if you want to make sure that someone does not open the back of a television set when it is connected to the power supply it would be much more effective to do this by some clearly readable sign

8-38

on the back of the set than by a note in the instructions. Undoubtedly, manufacturers need to give urgent attention to this question.

Safety is of course an evolving concept. This is clearly illustrated for instance in relation to motor cars where many modern cars have features which would have been unthinkable 30 years ago. Similarly, today, expensive cars have features, such as special braking systems, which are not to be found in cheaper cars. In the case of a car which is very likely to be in circulation for 10 and maybe for 20 or 30 years, a critical question is the time at which safety is to be tested. From the point of view of the producer, the critical time is when the goods are put into circulation. So a car sold for the first time in 1970 should be judged by 1970 and not by 1990 standards.

8-39   Manufacturers are not permitted to seek to contract out of liability under the Act but they may rely on the plaintiff's contributory negligence as reducing, or in extreme cases extinguishing, liability. Claims will be subject to the normal periods of limitation; that is that the actions must be brought within the appropriate time from the time the injury is suffered but, in addition, no action may be brought more than 10 years after the goods have first been put into circulation. In order to take full advantage of this defence, manufacturers will need to be able to prove when the particular article which has done the damage was put into circulation. The Act contains a number of defences. Of these, the most controversial is the so called 'development risk' defence under which the Act provides:

> '... that the state of scientific and technical knowledge at the relevant time was not such that the producer of products of the same description as the product in question might be expected to have discovered the defect if it had existed in his products while they were under his control.'

In effect, this reintroduces, by way of defence, a plea that the defendant was not negligent though with the burden of disproving negligence being on the producer. This defence will not be relevant where what has happened is a miscarriage of a normally safe production process or where the danger arises from inadequate warnings. It will be very important, however, where the allegation is that the producer has brought forth a new product which is unsafe. This can be perhaps most easily illustrated in relation to pharmaceuticals which is one of the areas where the defence will be most important. Under the pre-Act law, the plaintiff has to prove that the manufacturer or distributor of a new drug has been negligent in putting or keeping it on the market. In practice, this involves seeking to establish that the manufacturer's testing either on animals or on humans during the clinical testing stage was not as careful as it should have been. This presents enormous practical and cost problems for a private individual. If the Consumer Protection Act had not contained the development risk defence, the plaintiff would simply have had to prove that the drug was dangerous and in the case of a drug like thalidomide that would have been relatively easy though a plaintiff would still have to prove that his or her mother had in fact taken thalidomide while she was pregnant (which can give rise to serious problems where the same drug is put on the market at the same time by different manufacturers under different brand names). Under the provision in the Act, manufacturers will have the possibility of establishing that in the light of scientific and technical knowledge at the relevant time, they could not have been expected to discover the defect. This brings the law quite close to where it was already in relation to new products of this kind. The great difference is that the burden of proof will be on the manufacturer. This will mean that in practice, it has to give evidence about the nature and extent of its research. In some cases, manufacturers may choose not to do this or at least to make better offers than they would have done under the pre-Act regime in order to try to avoid having to do this.

6 CRIMINAL LIABILITY

Many of the changes which have taken place in the law discussed in this chapter in recent years have been driven by consumerism, that is the development of consumers as an organised group able to lobby for laws which protect their interests. One of the major problems with protecting the consumer is that changes in the substantive law of contract and tort do not help very much if the sums at issue are small and the cost of using lawyers is large. One way of dealing with this has been to provide special systems for trying small consumer cases in county courts from which lawyers are excluded. Another important development has been the building up of criminal law in the field of consumer protection. The great advantage of this from the consumer's point of view is that it has no cost since the operation of the criminal law is a service provided by the state. The disadvantage is that usually one does not receive financial compensation for one's own particular loss, though in certain cases the courts have been given power in the course of criminal proceedings to make compensation orders for those who have been injured by criminal trading behaviour. Nevertheless, at the prevention level, it is clear that the criminal law is of fundamental importance. Dishonest secondhand car dealers are much more likely to refrain from turning back the mileometers of cars they sell because of the fear that they may be caught and prosecuted than because of the fear that a customer to whom they sell a car will sue.

The notion that criminal law had a role to play in the fair regulation of the market is very old since it goes back to rules designed to produce fair weights and measures which have existed since medieval times. Again it is not possible to do more here than pick out a few salient points.

The most important Act in practice is the Trade Descriptions Act 1968 which gives rise to over 30,000 prosecutions a year. This makes it a criminal offence to apply a false trade description to goods in the course of a trade or business or to offer to supply any goods to which a false trade description is applied. The concept of trade description is very wide and has been treated as embracing eulogistic statements such as describing a car as a beautiful car or in 'immaculate condition' which would probably be regarded as not giving rise to liability in contract at all. Section 11 contains elaborate provisions about false or misleading indications as to the price of goods which have been replaced by Part III of the Consumer Protection Act 1987. Section 20(1) of that Act introduces a general offence of giving misleading price information and establishes a code of practice.

Another important step is to take power to prevent certain kinds of dangerous goods coming on the market at all. Extensive powers are granted to Ministers to make orders under the Consumer Protection Act 1961 and the Consumer Safety Act 1978. This has been used to regulate such matters as unsafe electric blankets and flammable nighties. Part II of the Consumer Protection Act 1987 introduces a general safety requirement which in s. 10(1) creates an offence if a person:

'(a)   supplies any consumer goods which fail to comply with the general safety requirements;

(b)   offers or agrees to offer to supply any such goods; or

(c)   exposes or possesses any such goods for supply.'

Under the Fair Trading Act 1973 the Director General of Fair Trading has important powers to promote fair trading practices. An important example of secondary legislation arising out of this Act is the Consumer Transactions (Restrictions on Statements) Order 1976 which prohibits traders from putting up notices which purport to exclude liability. As we shall see in the next chapter, there have been important changes in the law of contract which have made many attempts to exclude liability ineffective. If matters stopped here, however, it would be open to a trader to put up a notice purporting to exclude liability hoping that many customers would not realise that it had no legal effect. Using the criminal law to prohibit putting up of the notice is therefore a very important reinforcing mechanism.

CHAPTER 9

EXEMPTION AND LIMITATION CLAUSES

1 INTRODUCTION

During the last 150 years English law has come, principally by means of developing the implied terms discussed in Chapter 8, to impose substantial obligations on the seller particularly as to the quality of the goods. A natural response of sellers is to seek to qualify these obligations by inserting into the contract terms which seek to exclude, reduce or limit liability. Over the last 50 years English law has come to impose very considerable restrictions on the ability of the seller to do this even where he or she can persuade the buyer to agree to a contract which contains such a clause or clauses. This chapter will be concerned with explaining the devices which have been developed for this purpose.

9-01

It is important, however, to start by emphasising that such clauses are remarkably heterogeneous in form. It would be a mistake to assume that the underlying policy questions in relation to all types of clause are identical. Most clauses operate so as to qualify the results of the seller breaking the contract. This may be done in a wide variety of ways.

(a) The contract may provide that none of the implied terms set out in Chapter 8 shall be implied.

(b) The contract may provide that if the seller breaks the contract its liability should be limited to a particular sum, say £100.

(c) The contract may provide that if the seller breaks the contract it should only be liable to replace or repair the goods.

(d) The contract may provide that the seller shall not be liable for particular kinds of loss. So, for instance, contracts often provide that the seller is not liable for consequential loss so that if it fails to deliver the goods it will not be liable for loss of profit which the buyer suffers through not having the goods.

(e) The contract may provide that if the buyer wishes to complain it must do so within, say, 14 days.

(f) The contract may provide that if the buyer wishes to complain it must do so by means of arbitration.

(g) The contract may provide that if the goods are defective the buyer is not to be entitled to reject them but only to have the price reduced, and so on.

9-02   On the other hand, a clause may operate to define what it is that the seller is agreeing to do. Suppose an auctioneer of horses says that one of the horses which is up for sale is 'Warranted sound except for hunting'. This could be regarded as excluding liability if the horse would not hunt but it is more properly regarded as making it clear that the seller is not assuming any liability for the soundness of the horse as a hunter though it is warranting that the horse is sound in other respects. This distinction is fundamental since there is a great difference between saying from the outset that one does not assume an obligation and accepting an obligation and then seeking to qualify the consequences of it. This distinction was recognised in a different context in *Renton v. Palmyra* (1957)[1] where the contract provided for timber to be carried from British Columbia to London but contained a clause permitting the master of the ship, in the event of industrial disputes in London, to discharge at the port of loading or any other convenient port. Because of a dock strike in London the master delivered the goods in Hamburg. The House of Lords held that in the circumstances delivery in Hamburg was a performance of the contract because, properly construed, the contract provided alternative means of performance and not an excuse for non-performance. This was important because the contract was subject to the Hague Rules which forbid most forms of contractual limitation on liability. It must be admitted that much more commonly courts have chosen to ignore this distinction and to assume that all clauses operate by way of defence, so as first of all to consider what the rest of the contract says and then to consider whether the clause is effective to qualify that obligation. The difference in approach is not merely technical because it colours the whole flavour of the process of interpretation.

Common law and statute have developed rules which control the ability of the parties to exclude or qualify liability. Although as regards contracts of sale the statutory regime is much more extensive and important it is convenient to consider the common law position first, both because it provides the historical context in which the statutory regime exists and also because in order to be valid a contractual exclusion clause must survive both the common law and statutory tests.

---

[1]   [1957] A.C. 149.

2 THE POSITION AT COMMON LAW

Is the excluding clause part of the contract?

This question is assumed to be easy to answer where there exists a contractual document which has been signed by the parties. In this position the basic rule is that the parties can be taken to have agreed to what the contract means even though they have never read it and would not understand it if they had. Some commentators have criticised this rule on the grounds that in many cases the agreement on which it is based is wholly artificial. It is no doubt true that those who sign contracts embrace a range from those who can understand nothing up to those who are perfectly familiar with the contract and understand precisely its legal effect. It is probably not sensible, however, to make the binding force of the contract turn on where in the spectrum particular contracting parties stand. To enquire into these questions on a regular basis would be to consume vast amounts of judicial time without any obvious benefit.

More difficult questions arise where there is no signed contract but it is argued that excluding terms have been incorporated into the contract by notices or the delivery of non-contractual documents like tickets. There is no doubt that in certain circumstances one can incorporate terms into a contract by displaying a notice at the point at which the contract is made or, as on the railway, by handing over a ticket which contains references to the contractual conditions. These conditions need not be set out in the ticket provided they are sufficiently identified. So almost ever since the railways began tickets have borne on the front the words 'For conditions see back' and on the back a reference to the company's timetable. In principle this is perfectly acceptable. Similarly, there is no reason why one of the parties should not say by notice or ticket that all the contracts it makes are subject to the rules of a particular trade association. The critical test was that laid down in *Parker v. South Eastern Railway* (1877)[2], that is, whether or not in the circumstances the delivery of the ticket is sufficient notice of the terms referred to on it. In principle, it appears that the standard of reasonable notice is variable, so that the more surprising the term, the greater the notice required. So in *Thornton v. Shoe Lane Parking* (1971)[3] the plaintiff wished to park his car in the defendant's multi-storey car park. Outside the park was a notice stating 'All cars parked at owner's risk'. The ticket she received

---

2   (1877) 2 C.P.D. 416.
3   [1971] 2 Q.B. 163.

contained references to terms displayed inside. Inside the car park there were notices which purported to exclude not only liability for damage to cars but also liability for damage to drivers. This is a much less common clause and the Court of Appeal held that in the circumstances the plaintiff was not bound by it because he had not been given adequate notice so that he could make a real choice whether to park his car in that car park or somewhere else. It was obviously an important part of this reasoning that whereas car parks very commonly carry notices excluding liability for damaged cars, it is much less usual for them to carry notices excluding liability for damage to drivers. In the later case of *Interfoto Picture Library v. Stiletto Visual Programs* (1988)[4] the Court of Appeal stated it as a general proposition that where contracts were made by processes which involved the delivery by one side to the other of standard printed terms, the author of the terms was under a general duty to draw to the attention of the other side any terms which were unusual. Of course it follows that in a contested case it may be necessary to produce evidence of what terms are usual in a particular profession, trade or industry.

Limitations imposed by the common law on the effectiveness of exemption clauses

9-04   The principal tool used by common law to control exemption clauses has been the process of construction, that is the process by which the court construes (decides the meaning of) the contract. Courts have traditionally approached this process of construction by making a number of assumptions. These assumptions may often overlap but are probably analytically distinct. So it is assumed that it is unlikely for one party to agree that the other party shall not be liable even where he or she is negligent; similarly it is thought that the more serious a breach of contract has been committed by one party, the less likely it is that the other party will have agreed in advance that such a serious breach does not matter. Indeed, it was thought during much of the 1960s and 1970s that if the breach was sufficiently fundamental even the clearest words could not exclude liability for it but this was eventually decided by the House of Lords to be a heresy. The thrust of both of these assumptions is that if one party wishes to exclude its liability for negligence or a serious breach of the contract it needs to say so in clear terms. Of course, in practice what that party wants to do is to make expansive promises in the big print and cut them down by 'weasel words' in the small print. Few car parks would think it good business to put a large sign over the

---

[4]   [1988] 1 All E.R. 348; [1989] Q.B. 433.

entrance saying 'Abandon hope all ye who enter here'; it is quite a different matter to put a wide exclusion clause in small print on the back of the ticket. A third assumption which overlaps with these two but may have separate application is the *contra proferentem* principle which says that if one party has drafted or is responsible for the drafting of a document and the document is ambiguous then any ambiguities should be resolved in favour of the other party. All three of these assumptions are perfectly sensible within their proper limits; undoubtedly courts have, from time to time, gone over the top and used the devices to reject the effect of excluding clauses, not because they were not clearly drafted but because the court did not like them. More recent decisions have suggested that now that there is the statutory regime described below it is much less appropriate than it was in the past to take these techniques beyond their proper limits. It has also been suggested by the House of Lords that the force of the presumptions does depend very considerably on the type of clause which is employed. So clauses which impose financial limits on liability should not be treated with the same degree of hostility as clauses which exclude liability altogether. (Of course, this distinction can hardly apply where the financial limit is so low as in effect to exclude liability altogether.)

It has also been said that where one party has only entered into the   **9-05** contract because he or she has been misled by the other about the effect of the exclusion clauses then the exclusion clauses are without effect. This principle would obviously apply where the misrepresentation was fraudulent but it seems to apply even if the misrepresentation was entirely innocent. So in *Curtis v. Chemical Cleaning and Dyeing Co.* (1951)[5] the plaintiff took a wedding dress to the defendant for cleaning. Usually at a dry cleaner one would simply receive some kind of ticket by way of receipt but this particular cleaner had documents headed 'receipt' which it was the practice to ask the customer to sign. The plaintiff asked the assistant what was in the document and was told that it excluded liability for certain risks, for instance, damage to the beads and sequins which were on the wedding dress. In fact the receipt contained a clause 'The Company is not liable for any damage, however caused.' The dress was in fact stained while being cleaned and the defendant sought to rely on the clause as a defence. The Court of Appeal held that it could not do so because of the misstatement by the shop assistant about the effect of the document. There was no evidence in the case as to the assistant's understanding of the document and it is obviously entirely possible that the assistant understood it no better than the customer. This does not appear to matter.

---

5   [1951] 1 K.B. 805.

It is not clear whether the principle that surprising clauses should be specifically drawn to the attention of the other party applies where the document is signed. The cases in which it has arisen have not been cases of signed documents but the underlying rationale would seem to be equally applicable in such a case.

3 STATUTORY CONTROL OF EXEMPTION AND LIMITATION CLAUSES

9-06   There is a history of statutory control of exemption clauses going back to the middle of the 19th century when there were controls over the terms on which carriers of goods could seek to exclude liability. It is only much more recently, however, that general statutory regulation of such clauses has become accepted as an appropriate technique. A major step was the Supply of Goods (Implied Terms) Act 1973 which made major changes in the possibility of excluding clauses in the fields of sale and hire-purchase. These changes were re-enacted but with major additions in the Unfair Contract Terms Act 1977. This Act has provisions dealing specifically with contracts for the supply of goods and also provisions of general application which may affect contracts for the supply of goods.

Unfair Contract Terms Act, ss. 6 and 7

9-07   Section 6 of the Act applies to contracts of sale and hire purchase. Section 7 of the Act applies to other contracts under which ownership or possession of goods passes. Both sections deal with clauses which seek to exclude liability for failure to transfer ownership and this has already been discussed in Chapter 6. The main thrust of the sections is in relation to the implied terms as to the quality of the goods. Section 6 lays down the same rule for contracts of hire-purchase as for contracts of sale. Section 7 lays down the same rules for other contracts under which ownership or possession is to pass. For simplicity of exposition the rest of this account talks of contracts of sale but there is a uniform regime for all of these contracts.

Section 6 divides contracts into two groups; those where the buyer is dealing as a consumer and those where it is not. Where the buyer is dealing as a consumer ss. 13, 14 and 15 cannot be excluded. If the buyer is not dealing as a consumer ss. 13, 14 and 15 can be excluded if the term satisfies the requirement of reasonableness. In effect, therefore, the implied terms become mandatory in consumer sales and even in commercial sales the seller will only be able to exclude them if he or she is able to satisfy a court that the term excluding or limiting liability was in all the circumstances, reasonable. The operation of this scheme obviously involves two questions:

(a) who is a consumer; and

(b) what is reasonable in this context?

The answer to the first question is to be found in s. 12 which provides:

'(1)   A part to a contract 'deals as consumer' in relation to another party if -

(a) he neither makes the contract in the course of a business nor holds himself out as doing so; and

(b) the other party does make the contract in the course of a business; and

(c) in the case of a contract governed by the Law of Sale of Goods or Hire Purchase, or by s. 7 of this Act, the goods passing under or in pursuance of the contract are of a type ordinarily supplied for private use or consumption.

(2)   But on a sale by auction or by competitive tender the buyer is not in any circumstances to be regarded as dealing as consumer.'

Setting aside then the special cases of auction and competitive tender which can never be consumer sales, we see that a consumer sale requires three elements: a consumer buyer, a non-consumer seller and consumer goods. So, a sale by one consumer to another is not for this purpose a consumer sale. In any case, of course, a consumer seller does not attract liability under s. 14 of the Sale of Goods Act. It is thought, however, that a consumer seller who seeks to exclude liability under s. 13 of the Sale of Goods Act would be subject to the test of reasonableness. There is no definition of consumer goods and there are obvious marginal cases - for example, someone who buys a van intending to use it as his or her means of family transport. It is thought that courts will take a broad view of consumer goods for this purpose. The most difficult question is whether the buyer is making the contract in the course of a business or holding himself or herself out as doing so. There are many cases where a buyer buys goods partly for business and partly for non-business use. A typical example is the purchase of a car by a self-employed person. It is very likely that such a person would use the car substantially for family and social purposes but it is also very likely that for tax reasons it would be bought through the business. Many commentators had assumed that this would have made the transaction a non-consumer transaction but the contrary view was taken by the Court of Appeal in *R & B Customs*

9-08

Brokers v. United Dominions Trust (1988)[6]. In this case the plaintiff was a limited company, owned and controlled by Mr and Mrs Bell. The company conducted the business of shipping brokers and freight forwarding agents. It decided to acquire a Colt Shogun four wheel drive vehicle which turned out to be defective. The question was whether the transaction was a consumer transaction, in which case the exclusion clauses in the defendant's standard printed form would be totally ineffective. The defendant argued that the transaction must be a business transaction because companies only exist for the purpose of doing business. (This is obviously a stronger case on this point than if the plaintiffs had not incorporated themselves but had simply done business as a partnership having no separate legal personality.) The Court of Appeal held, however, that the company was a consumer and not a business for the purpose of s. 12. The principal reason for this decision was that the company was not in the business of buying cars. This decision has attracted a good deal of criticism since it appears to fly in the face of the wording of the Act (in particular it is difficult to see what effect can be given with this approach to the words 'nor holds himself out as doing so'). It is also very difficult to see how the regularity with which the plaintiffs bought cars was relevant to the character of the plaintiffs as consumers or non-consumers. Nevertheless, sellers would be prudent to assume that the decision is likely to be followed and its effect is clearly significantly to widen the notion of what is a consumer for this purpose.

9-09   The second question is what is reasonable? Section 11(1) says that whether the term is reasonable depends on:

'Having regard to the circumstances which were, or ought reasonably to have been, known to or in the contemplation of the parties when the contract was made'.

At the time when the Act was passed there was a debate about whether reasonableness should be determined at the time the contract was made or at the time the dispute arose. The Act adopts the former solution but in practice of course, the question will not arise until there has been a breach of contract and a dispute. The court will, in practice, be able to approach the question in the context which has actually arisen. This provision is less important in practice than it is in theory.

Section 11(4) provides:

'Where by reference to a contract term or notice a person seeks to restrict liability to a specified sum of money, and the question arises (under this or any other Act) whether the term or notice satisfies the requirement of reasonableness, regard shall be had in particular (but without prejudice to sub-section (2) above in the case of contract terms) to:

---

[6]   [1988] 1 All E.R. 847.

(a) the resources which he could expect to be available to him for the purpose of meeting the liability should it arise; and

(b) how far it was open to him to cover himself by insurance.'

This provision gives statutory force to the general notion that a clause limiting liability has a better chance of being treated as reasonable than a clause which seeks to exclude liability altogether. But this is only the case under s. 11(4) if the seller can show that the limit of liability is reasonably related to the resources which he or she has available. In other words, a small business can more readily defend a low limit of liability than a large one. However, many liabilities are, of course, insured and it is therefore relevant to consider whether the seller can cover himself or herself by insurance. In general, it is difficult for sellers effectively to insure against the cost of replacing the goods but they can insure against the possibility of having to pay damages for loss caused by defective goods. However, such insurance is commonly written with a premium which is calculated in relation to the maximum which the insurer will cover. It would seem that it is probably open to a seller to show that it was not economically possible for him or her to insure for liability for more than, say, £100,000 for any one claim. This would be relevant to the decision as to whether limitation of liability was reasonable under s. 11(4).

The court is also required to have regard to five guidelines which are set out in the second schedule to the Act. These are:

'(a)   the strength of the bargaining positions of the parties relative to each other, taking into account (among other things) alternative means by which the customer's requirements could have been met;

(b)   whether the customer received an inducement to agree to the term or in accepting it had an opportunity of entering into a similar contract with other persons, but without having to accept a similar term;

(c)   whether the customer knew or ought reasonably to have known of the existence and extent of the term (having regard, among other things, to any custom of the trade and any previous course of dealing between the parties);

(d)   where the term excludes or restricts any relevant liability if some condition is not complied with, whether it was reasonable at the time of the contract to expect that compliance with that condition could be practicable;

(e)   whether the goods were manufactured, processed or adapted to the special order of the customer.'

9-10   We may offer some comments on the guidelines. Obviously as far as (a) is concerned the more equal the bargaining position of the parties the more likely it is that the court could be persuaded that the clause is reasonable. Similarly, if one party is in a monopoly position it is likely to have considerable difficulty in persuading the court that the terms are reasonable, whereas if there is a wide range of possible suppliers this is likely to point in the other direction and particularly if some of them offer more favourable terms. There is an overlap here with (b), so that if a buyer has a choice of paying a higher price and getting a contract without exclusion clauses, whether that is from the same seller or different sellers the buyer who chooses the lower price may find that the clause is regarded as reasonable.

Guideline (c) calls for some comment. If the term is incorporated in the contract it must, in some sense, be the case that the buyer knows or has the opportunity of knowing it. It seems clear that more is required for the guideline to apply. It is thought that what is envisaged here is the case of an experienced buyer who knows the terms common in a particular trade and is not taken by surprise by them. (The reasoning in the *Stilleto* case above is obviously relevant here.) An example of the application of guideline (d) would be where the contract requires the buyer to complain of defects in the goods within a short period. Such a requirement might well be held reasonable in regard to defects which are obvious on delivery, particularly if the goods are to be delivered by a third party carrier, since notice may enable the seller to claim against the carrier. On the other hand, such a clause would usually not be reasonable if the defect was not immediately obvious[7].

9-11   The guidelines do not exhaust the factors which may be taken into account in deciding on what is reasonable. The leading decision is *George Mitchell (Chester Hall) Ltd. v. Finney Lock Seeds Ltd.* (1983)[8]. In this case the defendant was a firm of seed merchants which agreed to supply the plaintiff, a farming concern, with 30 pounds of Dutch winter cabbage seed for £192. The contract was treated as subject to an invoice which contained a clause purporting to limit liability if the seed were defective to a replacement of the seed or refund of the price and to exclude:

> 'All liability for any loss or damage arising from the use of any seeds or plants supplied by us and for any consequential loss or damage arising out of such use ... or for any other loss or damage whatsoever.'

---

[7]   *R W Green Ltd . v. Cade Bros. Farm* [1978] 1 Lloyds Rep. 602.
[8]   [1983] 1 All E.R. 10; [1983] 2 A.C. 803.

In fact, the seed delivered was not winter cabbage seed and was also defective. The plaintiff's crop was therefore a total failure. The plaintiff claimed that the cash value of the crop would have been some £63,000. The defendant claimed to be liable only to repay £192. If one looks at the guidelines in such a case, guidelines (b), (d) and (e) have little or no impact; there is probably not much to choose in the bargaining strength of the parties and clauses of this kind are well known in the seed trade so that it is unlikely that the reasonable farmer would be taken by surprise. On the other hand, it might be difficult to find a seed merchant who would supply a seed on substantially different terms.

The House of Lords held that the clause was unreasonable. The principal factor relied on by the House of Lords was that the defendant had led evidence that in practice in such cases it commonly made *ex gratia* payments. The purpose of leading this evidence was to show that the defendant was reasonable. Instead, the House of Lords took it as evidence that even the defendant did not regard its own clause as reasonable. These rather special circumstances are perhaps unlikely to arise again because in future sellers will not be so incautious as to lead such evidence. Other factors to which significant weight was attached included the fact that the breach by the sellers was a particularly clear and substantial one and that there was evidence that it was easier for sellers to insure against losses of this kind than for buyers. Undoubtedly, which parties can most economically and efficiently insure is often a critical factor in deciding whether a clause is reasonable. So if a seller could show that a particular loss was of a kind against which buyers commonly insure this would significantly increase his or her chances of persuading a court that the clause was reasonable[9]. Similarly, if the task being undertaken is relatively simple and its consequences fall within a modest compass it will be less easily shown to be reasonable to seek to exclude liability[10].

Another interesting case which is worth mentioning is *Walker v. Boyle* (1982)[11] where Dillon J held that neither the fact that the contract (for the sale of land) was on standard nationally used terms, nor the fact that both parties were represented by solicitors throughout, prevented the clause being unreasonable. This was because the clause in question sought to shift from seller to buyer the risk of the seller giving an inaccurate answer to questions, the answers to which were entirely within the seller's control.

---

9 *Smith v. Eric S Bush* [1990] 1 A.C. 831; [1989] 2 All E.R. 514.

10 *ibid.*

11 [1982] 1 All E.R. 634; [1982] 1 W.L.R. 495. This was a case on the Misrepresentation Act 1967 but it is thought that the reasoning applies equally to the Unfair Contract Terms Act.

Unfair Contract Terms Act, s. 2

9-12   Section 2 provides:

'(1)   A person cannot by reference to any contract term or to a notice given to persons generally or to particular persons exclude or restrict his liability for death or personal injury resulting from negligence.

(2)   In the case of other loss or damage, a person cannot so exclude or restrict his liability for negligence except in so far as the term or notice satisfies the requirement of reasonableness.

(3)   Where a contract term or notice purports to exclude or restrict liability for negligence a person's agreement to or awareness of it is not of itself to be taken as indicating his voluntary acceptance of any risk.'

Although this section is aimed at liability in negligence it is capable of applying to sellers and other suppliers of goods because in some cases the buyer may be able to formulate a claim against them as based on negligence. For instance, where the seller has negligently given pre-contract advice or, as discussed above, has carried out a negligent pre-delivery inspection of a motor car. It will be seen that s. 2 forbids contracting out of liability when negligence causes death or personal injury and subjects contracting out for negligence which causes other forms of loss to the test of reasonableness. What is said above about reasonableness will apply here also. Strictly speaking the Act provides that the guidelines should only be taken into account in respect of ss. 6 or 7 of the Act. However, in practice it seems that the courts have had regard to guidelines whenever questions of reasonableness arise. It would really be absurd to try to operate two different tests of reasonableness under the same Act.

Unfair Contract Terms Act, s. 3

9-13   Section 3 provides:

'(1)   This section applies as between contracting parties where one of them deals as consumer or on the other's written standard terms of business.

(2)   As against that party, the other cannot be reference to any contract term:

(a) when himself in breach of contract, exclude or restrict any liability of his in respect of the breach; or

(b) claim to be entitled:

(i) to render a contractual performance substantially different from that which was reasonably expected of him; or

(ii) in respect of the whole or any part of his contractual obligation, to render no performance at all except in so far as (in any of the cases mentioned above in this sub-section) the contract term satisfies the requirement of reasonableness.'

This provision is of very general scope. It will be seen that it applies either where one of the contracting parties is a consumer or where the contract is on one party's written standard terms of business. Obviously, there will be very many contracts of sale where the buyer is a consumer and many, both commercial and consumer contracts, where the contract is on the seller's standard written terms of business. So, many contracts of sale will be subject so s. 3. This section is therefore very important in relation to obligations under contracts of sale other than those covered by the implied terms in ss. 13, 14 and 15. It would apply, for instance, to the questions of when the seller is to deliver the goods. Many sellers state in their written standard terms of business that the dates of delivery are estimates only and so on. It would certainly be open to a court to enquire whether such a provision was reasonable. In practice it is very difficult to see that it can be reasonable simply to have a blanket excuse for being late in delivery. It would be a different matter if the seller inserted a clause excusing failure to deliver on time for specified events which were outside the seller's control. Such clauses are, of course, very common and in principle they would appear reasonable.

It should be noted that the scope of s. 3 is potentially very wide **9-14** because it covers not only attempts to exclude liability for breach of contract but also attempts to provide in the contract to be able to deliver a contractual performance substantially different from that which was reasonably expected or to render no performance at all. A careful draftsman might seek to formulate the contract so as to give the seller the right to offer an alternative performance or in certain circumstances not to perform at all without these acts being breaches but it seems that such clauses would still be subject to the test of reasonableness. If one applied this literally it would mean that a clause, providing that the seller need not deliver the goods until the buyer had paid for them in advance, was subject to the test of reasonableness. In practice it is unlikely that a court would be at all anxious to construe the words in this sense and in any case it would usually hold that such a clause was reasonable.

The Directive on Unfair Terms in Consumer Contracts was adopted **9-15** by the Council of Ministers on 5 April 1993. Member States were required to implement its provisions by 31 December 1994. The Directive was not mandatory as to its precise terms; it laid down a minimum standard which Member States must reach for protection of consumers against unfair terms in consumer contracts. Most Member States of the European Union already had legislation in place which deals with this area. In the case of the United Kingdom, the relevant legislation is the Unfair Contract Terms Act 1977. The Act is both wider and narrower than the Directive. It would have been possible for the Government to identify those areas at which the Directive is aimed, which the Act has not reached and to legislate to expand consumer protection to these areas. The Government decided not to do this and instead to introduce secondary legislation under s. 2(2) of the European Communities Act 1972.

The Unfair Terms in Consumer Contracts Regulations were laid before Parliament on 14 December 1994 and come into force on 1 July 1995.

To what contracts do the Regulations apply?

9-16   The Regulations apply only to consumer contracts; only to standard forms of contract; and only to contracts for the supply of goods and services. Let us consider each of these limitations in turn.

Although the concept of consumer contracts is used in the Act, it is clear that the Act is much wider in scope. It should be noted also that the Regulations define a consumer as 'a natural person who in making a contract to which these Regulations apply, is acting for purposes which are outside his business'.

The Regulations do not apply to contracts which have been individually negotiated. They are limited to contracts which have been 'drafted in advance'. Of course, it is extremely common in consumer contracts, if there is a written document, for the document to have been drafted in advance by the businesses' advisers. Nevertheless, even in such contracts there may be some negotiation, particularly about the price. The Regulations say that 'the fact that a specific term or certain aspects of it have been individually negotiated does not exclude the application of the Regulations if an overall assessment of the contract indicates that it is nevertheless a pre-formulated standard contract'.

The Regulations apply only to contracts for the supply of goods and services. The limitation to consumer contracts would exclude most international sales.

The effect of the Regulations

Under the Regulations, terms classified as unfair are struck out and in principle the rest of the contract would be left in being unless the effect of striking out the offending term is to leave a contract which makes no sense. There are two important differences between the Act and the Regulations here. The first is that, despite its name, the Act is not concerned with unfair terms. Whether a term is unfair is never a test of its validity under the Act. Some terms are simply struck out. Other terms are valid if reasonable. Invalidity does not depend on fairness or unfairness.

The second difference is that, subject to arguments about the precise scope of s. 3, the Act only applies to clauses which seek to exclude or limit liability. In principle, the Regulations can be used to attack any term which can be argued to be unfair.

Unfairness under the Regulations

Clause 5(1) of the Regulations provides that 'an unfair term in a contract concluded with a consumer by a seller or supplier shall not be binding on the consumer' and 5(2) 'the contract shall continue to bind the parties if it is capable of continuing in existence without the unfair term'. Unfairness is defined by Clause 4(1) of the Regulations which provides '"unfair term" means any term which, contrary to the requirement of good faith, causes a significant imbalance in the parties' rights and obligations arising under the contract to the detriment of the consumer.' So the possible scope of arguments about unfairness is very wide. However, there is one very important limitation which is contained in Clause 3(2) which provides 'In so far as it is in plain intelligible language no assessment shall be made of the fairness of any term which (a) defines the main subject matter of the contract or (b) concerns the adequacy of the price or remuneration as against the goods or services sold or supplied.' This means that it will not be open to a consumer to argue that a contract is unfair because he or she has been charged too much. This provision represents a vital decision as to a central part of the application of the unfairness concept. It is perfectly easy to understand why it was thought not expedient to leave judges with the task of deciding whether the price was fair. This would be the sort of question which could often not be answered without hearing complex economic evidence of a kind which many lawyers and judges are not trained to evaluate. On the other hand, questions of price must often be an important ingredient in questions of fairness and unfairness. Supposing I sell you a car which has been badly damaged in an accident, requires extensive repair work and is totally unroadworthy as it stands.

If I sell you the car at a price which reflects all these defects, it is hard to say that the contract is unfair. If I sell you the car at a price which would be appropriate for the same car in perfect second hand condition but seek to conceal the defects and to exclude liability by the words in the small print, it is much more plausible to regard the contract as unfair.

The Regulations give quite a lot of guidance as to what is good or bad faith. The second schedule requires particular regard to be had to 'the strength of the bargaining positions of the parties; whether the consumer has an inducement to agree to the terms; whether the goods or services were sold or supplied to the special order of the consumer; and the extent to which the seller or supplier has dealt fairly and equitably with the consumer'. It will be seen that the first three of these conditions are also relevant to reasonableness under the Act.

Section 6 of the Regulations provides 'A seller or supplier shall ensure that any written term of a contract is expressed in plain intelligible language'. Where 'there is doubt about the meaning of a term, the interpretation most favourable to the consumer shall prevail'. The second sentence is simply a statement in statutory form of a rule which the English courts have always applied and which indeed is to be found in virtually all legal systems. The wording of the first sentence of s. 6 is however of great practical importance. Many businesses operate at the moment by making glowing statements in their marketing and trying to weasel out of them in the small print by obscure and complex jargon. Section 6 will make this ineffective and certainly therefore requires consumer contracts to be carefully re-read and in many cases extensively re-written.

Finally, it should be noted that s. 4(4) provides that s. 3 contains 'an indicative and non-exhaustive list of the terms which may be regarded as unfair'. There is no corresponding list in the Act but such lists are a common feature of continental legislation. It should be noted that the list is not a black list in that the Regulations do not say in terms that inclusion on the list means that the clause is unfair. It is rather a grey list in the sense that inclusion on the list raises a strong inference that in most circumstances a clause of this kind should be treated as unfair.

Terms referred to in s. 4(4)

1. *Terms which have the object or effect of:*

    (a) excluding or limiting the legal liability of a seller or supplier in the event of the death of a consumer or personal injury to the latter resulting from an act or omission of that seller or supplier;

(b) inappropriately excluding or limiting the legal rights of the consumer vis-à-vis the seller or supplier or another party in the event of total or partial non-performance or inadequate performance by the seller or supplier of any of the contractual obligations, including the option of offsetting a debt owed to the seller or supplier against any claim which the consumer may have against him;

(c) making an agreement binding on the consumer whereas provision of services by the seller or supplier is subject to a condition whose realisation depends on his own will alone;

(d) permitting the seller or supplier to retain sums paid by the consumer where the latter decides not to conclude or perform the contract, without providing for the consumer to receive compensation of an equivalent amount from the seller or supplier where the latter is the party cancelling the contract;

(e) requiring any consumer who fails to fulfil his obligation to pay a disproportionately high sum in compensation;

(f) authorising the seller or supplier to dissolve the contract on a discretionary basis where the same facility is not granted to the consumer, or permitting the seller or supplier to retain the sums paid for services not yet supplied by him where it is the seller or supplier himself who dissolves the contract;

(g) enabling the seller or supplier to terminate a contract of indeterminate duration without reasonable notice except where there are serious grounds for doing so;

(h) automatically extending a contract of fixed duration where the consumer does not indicate otherwise, when the deadline fixed for the consumer to express this desire not to extend the contract is unreasonably early;

(i) irrevocably binding the consumer to terms with which he had no real opportunity of becoming acquainted before the conclusion of the contract;

(j) enabling the seller or supplier to alter the terms of the contract unilaterally without a valid reason which is specified in the contract;

(k) enabling the seller or supplier to alter unilaterally without a valid reason any characteristics of the product or service to be provided;

(l) providing for the price of goods to be determined at the time of delivery or allowing a seller of goods or supplier of services to increase their price without in both cases giving the consumer

the corresponding right to cancel the contract if the final price is too high in relation to the price agreed when the contract was concluded;

(m) giving the seller or supplier the right to determine whether the goods or services supplied are in conformity with the contract, or giving him the exclusive right to interpret any term of the contract;

(n) limiting the seller's or supplier's obligation to respect commitments undertaken by his agents or making his commitments subject to compliance with a particular formality;

(o) obliging the consumer to fulfil all his obligations where the seller or supplier does not perform his;

(p) giving the seller or supplier the possibility of transferring his rights and obligations under the contract, where this may serve to reduce the guarantees for the consumer, without the latter's agreement;

(q) excluding or hindering the consumer's right to take legal action or exercise any other legal remedy, particularly by requiring the consumer to take disputes exclusively to arbitration not covered by legal provisions, unduly restricting the evidence available to him or imposing on him a burden of proof which, according to the applicable law, should lie with another party to the contract.

2.   Scope of subparagraphs (g), (j) and (l)

(a) Subparagraph (g) is without hindrance to terms by which a supplier of financial services reserves the right to terminate unilaterally a contract of indeterminate duration without notice where there is a valid reason, provided that the supplier is required to inform the other contracting party or parties thereof immediately.

(b) Subparagraph (j) is without hindrance to terms under which a supplier of financial services reserves the right to alter the rate of interest payable by the consumer or due to the latter, or the amount of other charges for financial services without notice where there is a valid reason, provided that the supplier is required to inform the other contracting party or parties thereof at the earliest opportunity and that the latter are free to dissolve the contract immediately.

(c) Subparagraphs (g), (j) and (l) do not apply to:

− transactions in transferable securities, financial instruments and other products or services where the price is linked to fluctuations in a stock exchange quotation or index or a financial market rate that the seller or supplier does not control;

− contract for the purchase or sale of foreign currency, traveller's cheques or international money orders denominated in foreign currency;

(d) Subparagraph (l) is without hindrance to price indexation clauses, where lawful, provided that the method by which prices vary is explicitly described.

CHAPTER 10

REMEDIES

1 GENERAL PRINCIPLES

This chapter is intended to discuss what remedies may be available **10-01** to either the buyer or the seller if the other party breaks the contract. The positions of buyer and seller in a contract of sale are not, of course, symmetrical; the seller's obligation is to deliver the goods and the buyer's obligation is to pay the price. The failure of the seller to deliver the goods or to deliver goods of the right quality and so on will have different results from the failure of the buyer to pay the price, and may call for some difference in remedies. Nevertheless, the remedies available to the parties do derive very largely from the general law of contract and it seems more convenient therefore to approach the problem first by considering the general principles and then by considering how the position of the buyer and seller may differ.

It is important to make clear from the beginning that there will be a number of cases in which the injured party has no effective remedy for the other party's breach. This is because the most usual remedy is damages to compensate for the financial loss flowing from the breach and it will quite often be the case that little or no financial loss has flowed. Suppose, for instance, that a seller has contracted to deliver 1,000 tons of coffee beans at £525 per ton on 1 January and fails to deliver them. The buyer's remedy, as we shall see, is primarily measured in terms of what it would cost the buyer to buy substitute goods on the market on that date. It may be, however, that the price has fallen and in that case the buyer will actually profit from the seller's failure to perform, though of course the buyer does not have to account to the seller for the profit! Even if the price remains steady, the buyer will only have lost the cost of going out to the market to buy substitute goods which will often not amount to much. So the buyer will be entitled to an action for nominal damages but perhaps not much more.

Let us consider in turn what the possible remedies are. One party **10-02** may be entitled to withhold performance until the other has performed. So if the seller has agreed to give the buyer credit the buyer is not obliged to pay until the seller has delivered the goods. In a sense the right to withhold performance is a right rather than a remedy but it is also often the most effective way of concentrating the mind of the other party. In certain circumstances, one party will be entitled not only to withhold performance but to bring the contract to an end - to terminate it. A particular and very important example of this is the buyer's right to reject the goods, though the right to reject the goods is not exactly the same as the right to terminate and is not subject to exactly the same rules. Withholding performance, termination and rejection are discussed more fully later.

In certain circumstances, one party may be entitled to get the contract specifically enforced. This is the standard remedy for contracts for the sale of land because, from an early time, English courts have taken the view that each parcel of land is unique and a disappointed buyer cannot simply be compensated by damages since he or she cannot go out and buy an identical parcel of land elsewhere. This explanation is no doubt stretched when confronted by a typical English modern housing development but it appears to remain intact. A buyer may be able to obtain specific performance of a contract for the sale of goods but this is very much more an exceptional remedy. The Sale of Goods Act does not contemplate an action for specific performance brought by the seller but it does provide that in certain circumstances the seller may bring an action for the price and though this action is historically different from the action for specific performance it produces, from the seller's point of view, many of the same consequences. Specific performance and the action for the price are discussed later under 'Specific enforcement'.

In practice, the most common remedy for breach of a contract of sale of goods will be an action for damages. If the contract has been broken by one party, the other party will always have an action for damages though, as pointed out above, the damages may only be nominal in amount. The critical question is how much can be recovered by a buyer or seller in an action for damages. This will be considered in detail later under 'Actions for damages'.

10-03   The remedies we have discussed so far are what we may call the standard remedies provided by the general law. However, the law permits the parties to make further provisions about remedies. We have already seen in Chapter 9 the rules which have developed where the contract seeks to limit the remedies which would normally be available. It is possible, on the other hand, to seek to extend the range of remedies. So the contract may provide that if the seller is late in delivering he or she shall pay so much a day by way of liquidated damages for each day of delay. Conversely, the contract may provide that the buyer is to pay a deposit or that he or she is to pay part of the price in advance. Some of these possibilities are so common that substantial bodies of rules have been developed about them. These will be discussed more fully later under 'Party provided remedies'. 'Sellers' remedies against the goods' discusses certain special remedies which the seller has against the goods where the buyer is insolvent. In practice, the seller's most effective remedy is to have retained ownership. That we have already discussed in Chapter 6.

2 WITHHOLDING PERFORMANCE, TERMINATION AND THE BUYER'S RIGHT TO REJECT

Withholding performance and termination are analytically separate but in practice there is a major degree of overlap. This is because the factual situations which lead one party to wish to withhold performance or to terminate are very similar. In practice, the threat by one party to withhold performance will either lead the other party to attend to his or her performance, in which case the contract will go on, or not, in which the case the innocent party would usually have to decide a little later whether to terminate or not. So litigation is much more commonly about termination but no doubt withholding performance takes place very often in practice and has the desired result.   **10-04**

A critical question in deciding whether one party is entitled to withhold performance is to consider what the contract says or implies about the order of performance. So, for example, s. 28 of the 1979 Act says:

> 'Unless otherwise agreed, delivery of the goods and payment of the price are concurrent conditions, that is to say, the seller must be ready and willing to give possession of the goods to the buyer in exchange for the price and the buyer must be ready and willing to pay the price in exchange for possession of the goods.'

So in this standard case, neither the seller nor the buyer can withhold performance; each must be ready and willing to perform his or her side if he or she is to call on the other side to perform. In practice, however, other arrangements about payment and delivery are often made. The buyer may agree, and commonly does in an international sale, to open a banker's letter of credit and it has commonly been held that in such a situation the seller's obligation to ship the goods is conditional upon the buyer having opened the letter of credit for the right amount and the right currency with the right payment periods and so on. So, if the buyer fails to do this, the seller can withhold performance[1]. Conversely, the seller may have agreed to give the buyer credit. Suppose an oil company agrees to supply a filling station with all its requirements of oil for three years, payment to be made seven days after delivery. It is not open to the oil company unilaterally to change the terms and insist on payment in

---

1   *W. J. & Co Ltd v. El Nasr Export and Import Co.* [1972] 2 Q.B. 189; [1972] 2 All E.R. 127.

cash, even if the buyer has broken the contract by not always paying within the seven day limit (*Total Oil (Great Britain) Ltd. v. Thompson Garages (Biggin Hill) Ltd.* (1972)[2]).

These results can be expressed by saying that the buyer's obligation to pay is conditional on the seller having delivered the goods or that the seller's obligation to ship the goods is conditional on the buyer having opened a letter of credit. The parties need not necessarily have explicitly said what the order of performance is to be; in these cases, the courts have effectively inferred the order of performance from the commercial setting. So, in the case of the banker's letter of credit, it is unreasonable to expect the seller to expose itself to the risks of shipping the goods if the letter of credit has not been opened.

10-05   If we turn to consider the circumstances in which one party may terminate the contract, general contract law uses two principal approaches. One, which has been heavily used in relation to the sale of goods, is to proceed in terms of classifying the term of the contract which has been broken. This approach postulates that there are certain terms of the contract, commonly called conditions, which are so important that any breach of them should entitle the other party to terminate the contract. It is for this reason that a buyer can reject goods for breach of description even though the breach appears in commercial terms to be quite trivial, as in *Arcos v. Ronaasen* and *Re Moore and Landaeur*, discussed above in Chapter 8. Many of the obligations which we have discussed in the preceding chapters are expressed as being conditions and so attract the operation of this rule. In addition, there seems to be no reason why the parties may not agree that other express terms of the contract are to be treated as conditions. Unfortunately, the word 'condition' is used by lawyers in so many different senses that it is not absolutely certain that a court will construe a statement that a particular obligation is a condition as producing this result, as is shown by the decision of the House of Lords in *Schuler v. Wickman* (1973)[3], where it was said to be a condition of the agreement that Wickman should visit each of the six largest United Kingdom motor manufacturers at least once every week for the purposes of soliciting orders on behalf of Schuler. The House of Lords held by a majority, Lord Wilberforce dissenting, that this was not intended to produce the result that Schuler could terminate the contract because of Wickman's failure to make one visit in one week to one of the manufacturers. One suspects that, in fact, that was exactly what it was intended to do but that the

---

2   [1972] 1 Q.B. 318.
3   [1973] 2 All E.R. 39; [1974] A.C. 235.

majority of the House of Lords regarded this as such a draconian remedy that it chose to read the contract differently. Nevertheless, in a document clearly drafted by a lawyer, it must usually be the case that if it says that a particular obligation is a condition, breach of it will be treated as giving rise to a right to terminate.

A second way of approaching the problem of termination is to ask how serious a breach of contract committed by the defendant is. Basically, there are two principal possibilities. One is that one party has behaved in such a way as to make it clear that it is repudiating its obligations under the contract. A party can do this either by explicitly repudiating or by doing something which is inconsistent with any continuing intention to perform the contract. A classic example, given the context, is the old case of *Frost v. Knight* (1872)[4] where the defendant, having agreed to marry the plaintiff upon the death of his father, broke off the engagement during the father's lifetime. It was held that the lady could sue for damages at once, even though the date for performance of the contract might be many years off because it was clear to a reasonable man that the defendant would not perform (actions for breach of promise of marriage were abolished in 1970, but the principle of the case is still of general application).

Of course, deciding whether a particular course of conduct amounts to an implicit repudiation of a party's obligations may raise difficult questions of judgment. This is particularly the case where a party does something which turns out to be a breach of the contract but which it claims it was contractually entitled to do. The difficulties can be seen by contrasting two decisions of the House of Lords. In *Federal Commerce and Navigation v. Molena Alpha* (1979)[5] there were disputes between ship owner and time charterer. The owner, acting on legal advice, instructed the master not to issue freight pre-paid bills of lading and to require the bills of lading to be endorsed with charter party terms. They told the charterer that they had given these instructions. It was eventually decided that although the owner believed it was entitled to take these steps, it was in fact not entitled to do so. The House of Lords held that the owner's statement that it was going to take these steps was, in the circumstances, a repudiation. On the other hand, in *Woodar Investment Development v. Wimpey Construction* (1980)[6], Woodar agreed to sell 14 acres of land to Wimpey, completion to be two months after the granting of outline planning permission or on 21 February 1980, whichever was earlier. Because of developments in the land market, Wimpey was

10-06

---

4   (1872) 7 Exch. 111.
5   [1979] A.C. 757.
6   [1980] 1 All E.R. 571; [1980] 1 W.L.R. 277.

anxious to escape from the contract if it could. It claimed to be entitled to do so on the basis of a right to rescind which was in the contract but which was eventually held not to cover the circumstances which in fact existed. In this case, the House of Lords held, though only by a majority of three to two, that this conduct was not repudiatory. It will be seen that in both cases one party claimed to be entitled to do something under the contract which in fact it was subsequently held not to be entitled to do. In the first case, this conduct was treated as repudiatory and in the second, it was not. The fact that two Lords of Appeal dissented in the second case shows, as will be apparent to the reader, that the cases are not easy to distinguish. The principal difference probably lies in the fact that in the *Federal Commerce* case the behaviour of the ship owner was immediately coercive of the charterer whereas in the *Woodar* case, Wimpey had perhaps said no more than it would not perform when the time came and there was plenty of time to resolve the question of whether Wimpey was in fact correct in its view of the contract without bringing the contract to an end.

10-07   A second class of case in which one party is entitled to terminate is where the other party has performed in such a defective way as effectively not to have performed at all. Of course, some defective performances may be treated as evidence of an intention to repudiate. The thrust of this argument, however, is that one party, although he or she is doing his or her best, is doing it so badly that the other party is entitled to treat the contract as at an end. Such a breach is often called a fundamental breach though, in fact, many other metaphors have been used to describe the quality of defective performance which produces this effect. What is quite clear is that if one is talking of defective performance, a serious defect is involved so that the other party is deprived of an essential part of what he or she entered the contract to obtain.

Whether one is talking in terms of breach of condition or in terms of repudiatory or fundamental breach, it is clear that the contract does not come to an end simply because one of these events takes place. In each case, the innocent party has a choice. It can treat the breach of condition, the repudiatory breach or the fundamental breach, as bringing the contract to an end or it can continue to call for performance of the contract. Of course, in practice it will often become clear that the contract breaker cannot or will not perform and persistence in this course will inevitably lead the innocent party, in the end, to bring the contract to an end but, as a matter of legal theory, the contract comes to an end as a result of the innocent party's decision to terminate, not as a result of the guilty party's breach. The most obvious practical importance of this is that the innocent party's decision not to terminate will often give the other party a second chance to perform his or her side of the contract properly. Where the innocent party does elect to terminate the contract, the contract is not treated as never having existed but as terminated from that moment so that existing contractual rights and duties are not expunged. It follows that the innocent party can terminate and also claim damages for breach of contract if damages have been suffered.

There are special rules about late performance. Although the rules are similar to those in relation to other forms of breach in that they distinguish between important late performance and cases where late performance, although in breach of contract, is relatively unimportant, they have developed in a slightly different way because this was an area where equity intervened so as, in certain circumstances, to grant specific performance of the contract to one party even though he or she was late in performing.

10-08

The modern position may be stated as follows. A late performance is always a breach of contract and will give rise to an action for damages for any loss which actually follows from the late performance (in practice, it is often very difficult to show any loss resulting from late performance). However, whether the contract can be terminated for late performance depends on whether 'time is of the essence of the contract'. Time may be of the essence of the contract either because the contract expressly says so (and many contracts do expressly say that time is or is not of the essence of the contract) or because the contract is of a kind in which the courts treat timely performance as being essential. In general, courts have treated timely performance of the obligation to deliver the goods by the seller as of the essence of the contract, at least in a commercial context, unless the contract expressly says that time is not of the essence. On the other hand, the buyer's obligation to pay the price is not treated as an obligation where time is of the essence unless the contract expressly says so.

Where time is not of the essence but one party is late in performing, the other party is said to be able to 'make time of the essence'. What this means is that the innocent party may say to the late performer that if performance is not completed within a reasonable time, he or she will bring the contract to an end. It is of the essence of this possibility that the further time given for the performance is reasonable in all the circumstances and a party choosing to do this would be well advised to err on the side of generosity.

We saw above that the parties may agree in the contract that a particular obligation is to be treated as a condition. Alternatively, the parties may provide in the contract that one party is to be entitled to terminate. Such provisions are, in fact, very common. Sometimes, the event which gives rise to the right to terminate may be a breach of contract which would not have entitled the party to terminate were it not for this provision. So, in many contracts which depend on one party

10-09

paying periodically, it is common to provide that failure to pay promptly entitles the other party to terminate, although a court would not usually hold that a single failure to pay promptly was either a repudiatory breach or a fundamental breach. In some cases, a party may contract for the right to terminate without there being any breach of contract by the other side. So, if the Government places an order for a new fighter aeroplane, it may provide in the contract that the whole project can be cancelled if at a later stage defence policy changes. This would be a perfectly rational contractual arrangement to make. One would expect such a contract to contain provisions that the supplier was to be paid for the work which he or she had actually done up to the time of cancellation but the contract might well exclude the profit which the supplier would have made if the contract had been carried forward to completion. Obviously, clauses of this kind require careful negotiation and drafting.

Where the contract contains provisions for termination for events which are not in fact breaches of contract justifying termination on general principles, it may be important whether the contract makes the obligation essential or simply gives rise to a right to terminate. This is illustrated by the important case of *Lombard North Central v. Butterworth* (1987)[7].

10-10   In this case the plaintiff had leased a computer to the defendant for a period of five years and the defendant had agreed to pay an initial sum of £584.05 and 19 subsequent quarterly payments of the same sum. As is usual in such agreements, there was a clause giving the plaintiff the right to terminate the agreement if the instalments were not punctually paid. The defendant made two punctual payments and four late payments and the plaintiff then terminated the agreement, recovered possession of the computer and sold it for £172.88. It was clear that the plaintiff was entitled to do this. The question was to what further damages it was entitled. In a number of earlier decisions, of which the most important was *Financings v. Baldock* (1963)[8], it had been held that in such circumstances the plaintiff could not recover damages for loss of the interest payments which would have been earned if the contract had run to its end because the termination of the contract arose out of the plaintiff's decision to exercise his contractual right to terminate and not out of the defendant's breach of contract. However, in the present case, the contract, although very similar to earlier contracts, contained an extra provision which stated that 'punctual payment of each instalment was of the essence of the agreement'. The Court of Appeal held that this made a fundamental difference since its effect was that each failure to

---

7   [1987] 1 All E.R. 267; [1987] Q.B. 527.
8   [1963] 1 All E.R. 443; [1963] 2 Q.B. 104.

pay promptly was not only an event entitling the plaintiff to terminate but was also a breach of condition. It was said to follow that the termination of the contract flowed not from the plaintiff's decision to exercise its rights but from the defendant having committed a fundamental breach of contract so that all the plaintiff's loss flowed from this. This case shows that large results can flow from small variations in the wording of the contract.

The buyer's right to reject the goods is in a sense simply an example of the right to withhold performance or to terminate. It may be only the withholding of performance because in a few cases the seller will be able to make a second tender of the goods. This would usually only be where he or she can make a second tender within the contractually permitted time for delivery. Suppose the contract calls for delivery in January and the seller makes a defective tender on 1 January; he or she may well be able to make an effective tender later in the month. Where, as will often be the case, the contract calls for delivery on a particular day and time is of the essence, this possibility will in practice not exist and then rejection of the goods will effectively terminate the contract. Since many of the seller's obligations are expressed to be conditions, the buyer will have the right to reject the goods for breach of condition in a wide variety of circumstances. These include:

(a) a delivery of less or more than the contract quantity or of other goods mixed with the contract goods, as discussed in Chapter 5;

(b) failure by the seller to perform his or her obligations as to title as discussed in Chapter 6; or

(c) failure by the seller to carry out his or her obligations as to the quality of the goods as discussed in Chapter 8.

The buyer will also often be able to reject the goods because delivery is late, as discussed above. There is a major difference, however, between the rules governing the buyer's right to reject goods for breach of condition and the general law about termination. Usually, an innocent party cannot lose the right to terminate the contract until it has discovered that it has got it. However, it is clear that in some circumstances the buyer may lose the right to reject for breach of condition through acceptance even though it does not know that it has the right to reject because it has not yet discovered the defect which gives rise to this right. This is because the buyer loses the right to reject the goods by acceptance and it is possible for acceptance to take place before the buyer discovers the defect in the goods. This is because under s. 35(1) one of the ways in which the buyer can accept the goods is to retain them after the lapse of a reasonable time and a reasonable time is held to run from delivery and not from discovering that the goods are defective. This is discussed more fully above under 'Acceptance' (Chapter 5). The right of rejection is modified by two provisions which are incorporated by virtue of s. 4 of the Sale and Supply of Goods Act 1994. The first of these is a new section 15A which provides:

'(1)   Where in the case of a contract of sale -

(a) the buyer would, apart from this subsection, have the right to reject goods by reason of a breach on the part of the seller of a term implied by section 13, 14 or 15 above, but

(b) the breach is so slight that it would be unreasonable for him to reject them,

then, if the buyer does not deal as consumer, the breach is not to be treated as a breach of condition but may be treated as a breach of warranty.

(2)   This section applies unless a contrary intention appears in, or is to be implied from, the contract.

(3)   It is for the seller to show that a breach fell within subsection (1)(b) above.

(4)   This section does not apply to Scotland.'

It is assumed that, for a consumer buyer, the right of rejection is of particular importance. The great attraction of rejection, from the consumer point of view, is that it avoids any need to resort to litigation and forces the seller to decide whether it is worthwhile litigating. It can be assumed that, in respect of all goods except cars, consumers will be extremely reluctant to litigate, whatever the defects. The right of rejection is therefore particularly important. It is assumed, on the other hand, that, in the case of commercial sales, a reduction in price will more often than not satisfy the buyer's legitimate demands, unless the defect is a serious one. It is open to a commercial buyer to bargain for s. 15A to be excluded. It must be noted that it will require some cases to be sure what exactly will count as a slight breach and when it will be unreasonable to reject the goods because of such a breach. There is a two-fold test here. The seller must show both that the breach is slight and that it is unreasonable, to reject. It is not to be assumed that, simply because the breach is slight, it will be unreasonable to reject.

Finally, the buyer is given slightly greater rights of rejection by a new s. 35A which provides:

'(1)   If the buyer –

(a) has the right to reject the goods by reason of a breach on the part of the seller that affects some or all of them, but

(b) accepts some of the goods, including, where there are any goods unaffected by the breach, all such goods,

he does not by accepting them lose his right to reject the rest.

(2)   In the case of a buyer having the right to reject an instalment of goods, subsection (1) above applies as if references to the goods were references to the goods comprised in the instalment.

(3)   For the purposes of subsection (1) above, goods are affected by a breach if by reason of the breach they are not in conformity with the contract.

(4)   This section applies unless a contrary intention appears in, or is to be implied from the contract.'

By virtue of this new section, the buyer does not lose the right to reject some goods as part of a parcel of goods which are defective because he has accepted other goods in the parcel which are not defective. Under the previous law, the buyer who had 1,000 tonnes of wheat delivered to him, of which 400 tonnes were defective and 600 tonnes alright, had the choices of either rejecting the whole 1,000 tonnes or accepting the whole 1,000 tonnes (in either case, he might claim damages). Under s. 35A he will now have the option, if he wishes, to reject 400 tonnes and keep the 600 tonnes which are of good quality. This seems an entirely sensible change.

3 SPECIFIC ENFORCEMENT

Section 52 of the Sale of Goods Act provides:

'(1)   In any action for breach of contract to deliver specific or ascertained goods the court may, if it thinks fit, on the plaintiff's application, by its judgment or decree direct that the contract shall be performed specifically, without giving the defendant the option of retaining the goods on payment of damages.

(2)   The plaintiff's application may be made at any time before judgment or decree.

(3)   The judgment or decree may be unconditional, or on such terms and conditions as to damages, payment of the price and otherwise as seem just to the court.'

10-12

It will be seen that this section talks only of specific or ascertained goods and the question of whether specific performance can be given for unascertained goods is considered below. As far as specific or ascertained goods are concerned, the section is in very broad terms. However, in practice the courts have been very slow to exercise the broad powers given by the section. The reason for this is they have usually taken the view that in a contract for sale of goods damages will be an adequate remedy since usually the buyer can go out and buy substitute goods and be adequately compensated by a money payment. So in *Cohen v. Roche* (1927)[9] the court refused specific performance of a contract for what was described as 'ordinary Hepplewhite furniture'. In 1990 there is perhaps not such a market for 'ordinary Hepplewhite furniture' that one can easily go out and buy substitutes and such a case would perhaps be close to the line. It was perhaps an important factor in the case that the buyer was buying the goods for resale. This greatly strengthened the argument that damages were an adequate remedy. A leading case in which specific performance was granted was *Behnke v. Bede Shipping* (1927)[10] in which the subject matter of the contract was a ship. It cannot be assumed, however, that specific performance would routinely be given even of contracts for the sale of a ship. So in *CN Marine v. Stena Line* (1982)[11], specific performance was refused of such a contract. A court would want to enquire, in any decision whether to grant specific performance, into all the circumstances, in particular on any hardship which would be caused to one party or the other by giving or refusing specific performance or the conduct of the parties leading up to the contract. This reflects a combination of two policies: the general feeling that specific performance is usually not necessary in the case of goods and the general equitable principle that specific performance is not to be granted mechanically and that all the circumstances are to be considered. Another recent case which illustrates the reluctance of the court to grant specific performance is the *Bronx Engineering* (1975) case[12], where the subject matter of the contract was a machine weighing over 220 tons, costing £270,000 and only buyable with a nine month delivery date.

10-13   As we said above, s. 52 only talks in terms of 'specific or ascertained goods'. This leaves in the air the question whether specific performance can ever be granted of unascertained goods. One view, which was discussed in Chapter 1, is that the Sale of Goods Act contains an exhaustive code of the remedies available. This view was expressed in relation to specific performance in *Re Wait* (1972)[13]. However, in the leading modern case where the question arose, the judge did, in fact, grant specific performance of a contract for unascertained goods though he did not refer to s. 52 or consider the theoretical question of whether

---

[9]   [1927] 1 K.B. 169.
[10] [1927] 1 K.B. 649.
[11] [1982] 2 Lloyd's Rep. 336.
[12] [1975] 1 Lloyd's Rep. 465.
[13] [1972] 1 Ch. 606.

he had jurisdiction. This was in *Sky Petroleum v. VIP Petroleum* (1974)[14]. In this case there was a contract for the supply of petrol to a filling station and the seller refused to deliver. Normally, no question of specific performance would arise on such facts because the filling station could go and buy petrol on the market and be compensated adequately by damages. However, at the time of the case, the Yom Kippur war had recently disrupted supplies of petrol so that alternative supplies were not available to the buyer. In the circumstances, specific performance was a uniquely desirable and effective remedy. The decision of the judge that he should give specific performance seems entirely sensible though it is perhaps unfortunate that he did not consider the theoretical question of whether he had power to do so.

Section 52 talks of plaintiffs and defendants and not of buyers and sellers. So it may be that in theory a seller can sue for specific performance. However, this is not likely to be a practical question except in the most extraordinary circumstances since a seller will nearly always be able to sell the goods elsewhere and recover compensation by way of damages for any loss that he or she suffers. There will be cases, however, where the seller would wish, if possible, to sue for the price rather than to sue for damages. This is principally because in the English system, actions for defined sums of money are much easier, quicker and therefore cheaper than actions for damages. Section 49 of the 1979 Act provides:

'(1)   Where, under a contract of sale, the property in the goods has passed to the buyer and he wrongfully neglects or refuses to pay for the goods according to the terms of the contract, the seller may maintain an action against him for the price of the goods.

(2)   Where, under a contract of sale, the price is payable on a day certain irrespective of delivery and the buyer wrongfully neglects or refuses to pay such price, the seller may maintain an action for the price, although the property in the goods has not passed and the goods have not been appropriated to the contract.'

Although the action for the price is in a sense the seller's equivalent   **10-14** of the buyer's action for specific performance, the two remedies should be kept clearly distinct. This is for historical reasons. The action for specific performance arises historically from the jurisdiction of the Court of Chancery to grant specific performance which was always said to be discretionary and to turn on taking into account all the relevant circumstances. The action for the price was not an equitable action but basically a common law action for debt. This means that where sellers

---

14   [1974] 1 All E.R. 954.

are entitled to sue for the price they do not have to show that they have suffered any loss; they do not have to take steps to mitigate the loss as they do in a damages action and the action is not subject to any general discretion in the court. On the other hand, the seller does not have an action for the price simply because the buyer's obligation to pay the price has crystallised and the buyer has failed to pay. The seller has to bring the case within one or other of the two limbs of s. 49.

It will be seen that s. 49(1) links the right to sue for the price to the passing of property. This is another example of the point discussed in Chapter 6 that the passing of property in the English system is largely important because of the other consequences which are made dependent on it. It will be remembered that whether property has passed is quite independent of delivery. So, in principle, a seller may be able to sue for the price because property has passed even though he or she still has the goods in his or her hands. Conversely, a seller who has delivered the goods but has provided that property is not to pass until he or she has been paid, as is of course common under retention of title clauses, cannot sue for the price under s. 49(1).

10-15   Section 49(2) provides an alternative basis for an action for the price where the price is payable 'on a day certain irrespective of delivery'. This clearly covers the simple case where the contract says that the price is payable on 1 January. It certainly does not cover the rather common case where the price is payable on delivery, even where the contractual date for delivery is agreed, because it can then be held that that is not a day certain irrespective of delivery; *Stein Forbes v. County Tailoring* (1916)[15]. What about the cases which fall in between these two extremes? It certainly seems that it will do if the parties agree a date even though at the time of the agreement neither of them knows when it is, such as on Derby Day 1991 or probably on some date which will become certain but is outside their control, such as the date of the next General Election. (These are no doubt not very likely practical examples!) An important practical test arose over *Workman Clark v. Lloyd Brazileno* (1908)[16]. This was a ship building contract under which it was agreed that the price was to be paid in instalments which were linked to the completion of various stages of the ship. Such provisions are extremely common in ship building contracts for obvious cash flow reasons. So, a ship building contract may well provide that 20% of the price is to be paid on the laying of the keel. Obviously, at the time of the contract, no-one will know exactly when the keel will in fact be laid, even if the contract contains provisions as to when it should be laid. Nevertheless, in the

---

[15] (1916) 86 L.J. K.B. 448.
[16] [1908] 1 K.B. 968.

Workman Clark case it was held that such provisions were for payment on a day certain because when the duty to pay arose, the day on which it fell due was certain. So, it would seem that in general it is sufficient that the day of payment is certain when payment falls due, provided that it is not delivery which makes it certain.

A question which has not been tested in litigation is whether the parties may extend the scope of s. 49 by agreement. A seller, for instance, might well wish to provide that property was not to pass until he or she had been paid but that he or she could sue for the price once the goods had been delivered. There does not seem to be any obvious reason why the parties should not be able to make an agreement to this effect.

4 ACTIONS FOR DAMAGES

The 1979 Act contains three sections which deal with damages. These are: **10-16**

'50. (1) Where the buyer wrongfully neglects or refuses to accept and pay for the goods, the seller may maintain an action against him for damages for non-acceptance.

(2) The measure of damages is the estimated loss directly and naturally resulting, in the ordinary course of events, from the buyer's breach of contract.

(3) Where there is an available market for the goods in question the measure of damages is prima facie to be ascertained by the difference between the contract price and the market or current price at the time or times when the goods ought to have been accepted or (if no time was fixed for acceptance) at the time of the refusal to accept.

51. ((1) Where the seller wrongfully neglects or refuses to deliver the goods to the buyer, the buyer may maintain an action against the seller for damages for non-delivery.

(2) The measure of damages is the estimated loss directly and naturally resulting, in the ordinary course of events, from the seller's breach of contract.

(3) Where there is an available market for the goods in question the measure of damages is prima facie to be ascertained by the difference between the contract price and the market or current price of the goods at the time or times when they ought to have been delivered or (if no time was fixed) at the time of the refusal to deliver.

53.   '(1) Where there is a breach of warranty by the seller, or where the buyer elects (or is compelled) to treat any breach of a condition on the part of the seller as a breach of warranty, the buyer is not by reason only of such breach of warranty entitled to reject the goods; but he may -

(a)   set up against the seller the breach of warranty in diminution or extinction of the price, or

(b)   maintain an action against the seller for damages for the breach of warranty.

(2) The measure of damages for breach of warranty is the estimated loss directly and naturally resulting, in the ordinary course of events, from the breach of warranty.

(3) In the case of breach of warranty of quality such loss is *prima facie* the difference between the value of the goods at the time of delivery to the buyer and the value they would have had if they had fulfilled the warranty.

(4) The fact that the buyer has set up the breach of warranty in diminution or extinction of the price does not prevent him from maintaining an action for the same breach of warranty if he has suffered further damage.'

10-17   In practice these provisions do not add a great deal to the general law of contract and many cases are decided without reference to them. It is more satisfactory, therefore, to start by setting out some general contractual principles about damages. For this purpose it is useful to start by considering what kinds of loss a buyer or seller may suffer as a result of the other party breaking the contract. For this purpose, English commentators have now largely adopted a distinction first drawn in a famous American Law Review article in 1936 between expectation loss, reliance loss and restitution loss[17]. This terminology is now beginning to be recognised by the English courts[18].

Expectation loss is the loss of what the injured party expected to recover if the contract was carried out. The great feature of the law of contract is that on the whole it is designed to protect people's expectations and a plaintiff should therefore normally be able to get damages which will carry him or her forward into the position which he or she hoped and expected to reach. So, in principle, if I order goods which I intend to use in my business for the purpose of making a profit, I

---

[17]   Fuller and Purdue 46 YALE L.J. 52.

[18]   *CCC Films (London) Ltd. v. Impact Quadrant Films Ltd.* [1985] Q.B. 16; [1984] 3 All E.R. 298.

should be able to recover damages for non-delivery of the goods which will compensate me for not having made the profit. Needless to say, this broad general principle is subject to qualifications which will appear later.

Cases may arise, however, in which it is very difficult for the plaintiff to prove, in any way which would be acceptable to a court, what his or her expectation loss would be but where it is clear that the plaintiff has suffered loss as a result of the contract having been broken. The plaintiff may seek to argue that he or she has suffered what is called reliance loss, that is loss arising out of having relied on the defendant honouring the contract. A good example is the case of *McRae v. Commonwealth Disposals Commission* (discussed above in Chapter 7). In this case, the plaintiff did not recover his expectation loss, that is the profit he would have made from recovering the tanker if it had existed, because this was too speculative to be established but he did recover his reliance loss, that is the cost of mounting the expedition to look for the tanker.

The general principle appears to be that the plaintiff has a free choice **10-18** whether to formulate the claim in terms of expectation loss or reliance loss unless the defendant can prove that the bargain that the plaintiff had made was such a bad one from the plaintiff's point of view that it would not even have recouped the reliance loss if the contract had been performed *CCC Films v. Impact Quadrant Films* (1984)[19].

A third form of loss which the plaintiff may have suffered is that he or she may have paid over money to the defendant in pursuance of a contract which has gone off, as for example where the purchaser has paid part of the price in advance and the seller has then failed to deliver the goods. In certain circumstances, the plaintiff will be able to sue simply to recover the money but this would not be part of a damages action but a separate action of a restitutionary kind.

The law does not say, whether the plaintiff is formulating the claim for expectation loss or for reliance loss, it can recover all its loss. The courts have said that some loss is too remote. It is at this question that s. 50(2) and s. 51(2) are aimed. It will be seen that those sections lay down the same test which is that the measure of damages is the estimated loss directly and naturally resulting, in the ordinary course of events, from the breach of contract. This is the draftsman's attempt to state the general contract law in the context of a failure by the seller to deliver the goods or by the buyer to accept them respectively. This rule is contained, for general contract law, in a series of cases of which *Hadley v. Baxendale* (1854)[20] is the earliest and still most famous and the *Heron II* (1969)[21] is

---

19 [1984] 3 All E.R. 298.
20 (1854) 9 Exch. 341.
21 [1969] 1 A.C. 3550.

perhaps the most important modern example. Both of those cases were concerned with delay in delivery by carriers but they lay down principles of general application. They do provide both an endorsement and a substantial addition to the test laid down in s. 50(2) and s. 51(2). They provide an endorsement because indeed a plaintiff can normally recover any loss which directly and naturally results, in the ordinary course of events. However, a plaintiff may also be able to recover loss which does not directly and naturally result provided that he or she has adequately informed the defendant before the contract is made of the circumstances which in the particular case made the loss a consequence of the defendant's breach of contract. It follows that a defendant cannot say that the loss is too remote if it flows either from the ordinary course of events or from circumstances which the defendant adequately knew about at the time the contract was made. It follows that in principle the more the defendant knows about the plaintiff's business, the greater the possibility that the plaintiff will be able to recover compensation for loss which flows from the defendant's breach of contract. In some cases, judges have described these results by using the language of foreseeability, though in the *Heron II* the House of Lords deprecated the use of that word which they thought more appropriate to the law of tort and suggested alternative formulations such as 'contemplated as a not unlikely result'.

10-19   It is important to make clear, however, that what the parties have to contemplate is the kind of loss which will be suffered and not its extent. So, if a seller fails to deliver, it is foreseeable that the buyer will have to go out and buy substitute goods. One of the ways of calculating the buyer's loss is to compare the contract price and the price that the buyer has actually had to pay. This is readily within the contemplation of the parties. It would make no difference that the price had gone up in a way which nobody could have contemplated at the time of the contract (*Wroth v. Tyler* (1974)[22]).

It is often said that the plaintiff must mitigate its damages. This is strictly speaking an inaccurate way of putting the point. The plaintiff can do what it likes but would only be able to recover damages which result from reasonable behaviour after the contract is broken. This is really an application of the general principle that the plaintiff can only recover what arises in the ordinary course of events and in the ordinary course of events those who suffer breaches of contract respond in a reasonable way (or at least the law treats them as if they will). This principle can be an important limitation on the amount that the plaintiff recovers. This is illustrated by the case of *Payzu v. Saunders* (1919)[23], where the defendant

---

[22] [1974] Ch. 30.
[23] [1919] 2 K.B. 581.

had agreed to sell to the plaintiffs a quantity of silk, payment to be made a month after delivery. The defendant, in breach of contract, refused to make further deliveries except for cash and the plaintiff treated this as being a repudiation and elected to terminate the contract. This they were certainly entitled to do. They then sued for damages on the basis that the market price of silk had risen and that they could claim the difference between the contract price and the market price at the date of the buyers' repudiation. This argument was rejected on the grounds that, the market having risen, it would have been cheaper for the buyers to accept the seller's offer to deliver against cash at the contract price. Of course, it will often be difficult for the plaintiff to know immediately after the contract what is the best course. In principle, if the plaintiff acts reasonably, it should be able to recover its financial loss even though, with the wisdom of hindsight, it appears that the plaintiff could have minimised the loss by doing something different (*Gebruder Metelmann v. NBR (London)* (1984)[24]).

How do we apply these general principles to the specific case of contract for the sale of goods? One answer is given by ss. 50(3) and 51(3) which, it will be seen, are in very similar terms. This states the market rule, to which several references have already been made. English litigation in the field of sale of goods has been dominated by commodity contracts where there is a national or international market and it is possible to say with precision what the market price is during the hours when the market was open. In such a situation it is assumed that if the seller refuses to deliver, the buyer will buy against the seller in the market or that if the buyer refuses to accept, the seller will sell against the buyer in the market and that the starting point for enquiry is the difference between the contract price and the market price. This is basically a very simple rule to apply and it is a useful example of the application of the general principle. The fact that it is the only specific case actually discussed in the Act perhaps, however, gives it more prominence than it really deserves. It should be emphasised that the rule does not apply where there is no 'available market' and even where there is an available market, the rule will not necessarily apply[25]. **10-20**

Whether the market rule is the right rule to apply will depend, amongst other things, on the nature of the loss suffered by the plaintiff[26]. This is shown by the case of *Thompson v. Robinson* (1955)[27]. In that case, the plaintiff was a car dealer which contracted to sell a

---

24 [1984] 1 Lloyd's Rep. 614.
25 There may be a market for goods of the contract description but not of the contract amount. For a solution of the consequential problems see *Shearson Lehman v. Maclaine Watson* [1990] 3 All E.R. 723.
26 *Sealace Shipping Co. v. Oceanvoice, The Alecos* [1991] 1 Lloyd's Rep. 120.
27 [1955] 1 All E.R. 154; [1955] Ch. 177.

Standard Vanguard car to the defendant who wrongfully refused to take delivery. At this time, there was effective resale price maintenance for new cars so that there was no difference between the contract price and the market price and the buyer argued that the plaintiff had suffered no loss. However, the plaintiff showed that in fact there was a surplus of Standard Vanguard cars and that it had therefore lost its profit on the deal which could not be replaced by selling the car to someone else since it had more cars than it could sell. In this case, the plaintiff's loss was the loss of the retail mark up, that is the difference between the price at which the car was bought from the manufacturer and the price at which it could be sold. Of course, if the dealer could sell as many cars as it could obtain, then it would not effectively have lost this sum, as was held in the later case of *Charter v. Sullivan* (1957)[28].

10-21   From the buyer's point of view a most important question arises where it wishes to argue that what has been lost is a particularly valuable sub-sale. Suppose A has contracted to sell to B for £100 and B has contracted to sell to C for £150. Suppose further that A fails to deliver in circumstances where B cannot buy substitute goods in time to perform his contract with C and loses his profit on the transaction. Can he recover the profit? If we were applying the standard rules, this would appear to turn either on whether this was a loss in the usual course of things, which it might well be if the buyer was a dealer since the sub-sale would then appear to be entirely usual, or where the buyer had told the seller of the sub-sale. In practice, the courts have been reluctant to go so far. The leading case is *Re Hall and Pims Arbitration* (1928)[29]. In this case, the contract was for the sale of a specific cargo of corn in a specific ship. The contract price was 51s 9d per quarter and the buyer resold at 56s 9d per quarter. The seller failed to deliver and, at the date when the delivery should have taken place, the market price was 53s 9d per quarter. Clearly the buyer was entitled at least to the difference between 51s 9d and 53s 9d per quarter but claimed that to be entitled to the difference between 51s 9d and 56s 9d, the price at which it had agreed to re-sell. It was held by the House of Lords that this was right. However, this was a very strong case for two reasons. The first was that both the sale and the sub-sale were of the specific cargo so that there would be no question of the buyer going into the market to buy substitute goods. The second was that the contract of sale between plaintiff and defendant expressly provided for re-sale by the buyer.

---

[28] [1957] 2 Q.B. 117.
[29] (1928) 1 39 L.T. 50.

Section 50 is concerned with the case where the buyer refuses to accept the goods and s. 51 with the case of the seller who fails to deliver. Of course, the seller can break the contract not only by failing to deliver but also by delivering late or making a defective delivery. This is dealt with by s. 53 which was set out above. It will be seen that again this sets out reliance on the market rule. It is clear, however, that there are many other forms of loss which may arise in the usual course of things. So, defective goods may cause damage to persons or property before their defects are discovered. Late delivery may cause loss of profit where the goods were to be used to make profits.

A major problem with all of these rules about damages is the extent **10-22** to which the plaintiff is seeking to recover his or her actual loss or what one might call his or her notional loss. In general, for instance, when one is applying the market rule it does not seem to matter whether the buyer has gone into the market and bought substitute goods or not. The buyer can recover the difference between the contract price and the market price even though he or she does not buy against the seller; conversely, the buyer cannot recover more than this where he or she has stayed out of the market until later and then had to buy back at a higher price. However, it seems that sometimes courts will look to see what actually happens. An important and difficult case is *Wertheim v. Chicoutimi* (1911)[30], where the seller delivered late. At the time when the goods ought to have been delivered, the market price was 70s a ton but by the time the goods were actually delivered, the market price was 42s 6d a ton. On the principles set out above, it would seem to follow that the buyer should have been able to recover the difference between 70s and 42s 6d for every ton he had contracted to buy. In fact, the buyer had managed to re-sell the goods at the remarkably good price in the circumstances of 65s a ton. It was held that he could only recover the difference between 70s and 65s for each ton bought. At first sight this looks reasonable since it might be said that this was the only loss which the buyer had actually suffered. On the other hand, the reasoning deprives the buyer of the profit to which his commercial astuteness at selling well over the market price would normally have entitled him. It is not surprising, therefore, that the correctness of this decision has been much debated.

5 PARTY PROVIDED REMEDIES

It seems, within broad limits, that parties have freedom to add on by **10-23** contract additional remedies. So, we have already seen earlier that the

---

[30] [1911] A.C. 301.

right to terminate may be extended by contract. Two other important additional remedies which should be mentioned are liquidated damages and deposits.

Many contracts of sale provide that, in the event of certain breaches, typically late delivery by the seller, he or she shall pay damages at a rate laid down in the contract, for instance £X for every day by which delivery is delayed. Such provisions have important practical advantages because, as noted above, it is very much easier to bring actions for defined sums of money. However, the parties do not have complete freedom as to what may be agreed in this area. Since the 17th century, the courts have distinguished between liquidated damages which are enforceable and penalties which are not. The distinction turns on whether the sum agreed is a reasonable pre-estimate as at the time of the contract of the amount of loss which is liable to flow from the contract being broken in the way contemplated. If the sum agreed is a reasonable pre-estimate, then it is classified as liquidated damages and is recoverable. If it is more than the reasonable pre-estimate then it is classified as a penalty and is not recoverable, leaving the plaintiff to recover such unliquidated damages as he or she can in fact establish. It is important to emphasise that the test is not the plaintiff's actual loss but the plaintiff's contemplated loss as at the time of the contract. So liquidated damages can be recovered even though there is no actual loss or less actual loss than the agreed sum, provided the pre-estimate was reasonable.

A contract may provide for the payment in advance by the buyer of sums of money. Here, the law has drawn a distinction between deposits and advance payments. In certain types of contract it is common for the payment to be made in stages, tied to the achievement of particular stages of work. So, as we saw above, in a ship building contract it would be common for there to be a payment of part of the price when the keel is laid. The purpose of these schemes is to help the seller with cash flow. It typically occurs in major capital contracts when the seller or supplier has to spend considerable sums of money on acquiring components and on fitting them together. Suppliers, typically, are unwilling to finance the whole of the cost of this and stipulate for payment in instalments tied, as we have said, to particular stages of completion.

10-24   On the other hand, the buyer may have paid a deposit so as to give the seller a guarantee that the buyer will in fact go through with the contract. So, the buyer may have gone into the seller's shop and picked some goods and said that he or she would like to buy them and would come back tomorrow to collect them. In certain trades it would be very common for the seller to take a deposit because sellers know from experience that many buyers do not return and they may lose the opportunity of selling the goods elsewhere.

The importance of the distinction is this. If, having paid money in advance, the buyer then breaks the contract, he or she will of course be liable to damages and if the damages exceed what has been paid in advance then it will simply be a question of the seller recovering the balance. But the seller's damages may be less than the deposit or advance payment. In this situation, the courts have said that the seller can keep the deposit even if the deposit is greater than the seller's actual loss whereas if there has been an advance payment which is greater than the seller's actual loss, the seller can only keep the actual loss and must return the balance.

The amount of the deposit may be not only greater than the seller's actual loss but than any loss to the seller greater than was reasonably foreseeable at the time of the contract. In such a case it might plausibly be argued that the deposit is in fact a penalty. In practice, however, courts have tended to keep the rules about penalties and deposits in watertight compartments. A marked change of attitude was revealed in the recent case of *Workers Trust and Merchant Bank Ltd. v. Dojap Investments Ltd.* (1993)[31] where the Privy Council was prepared to treat a deposit in a contract for the sale of land as penal where it exceeded the going rate (10%) (of course even a deposit of 10% might exceed any likely loss but it was effectively held that it was too late to question the taking of deposits at the going rate).

6 SELLERS' REMEDIES AGAINST THE GOODS

The seller's principal concern is to ensure that he or she is paid for the goods. The most effective and common way of doing this is for the seller to retain ownership of the goods as long as possible. We have already discussed this in Chapter 6. The Act does, however, give the unpaid seller further rights in relation to the goods as well as his or her right to sue the buyer for the price or damages. The provisions which are contained in ss. 38 to 48 of the Act are complex but do not appear to be of much practical importance in modern situations. The central provision is s. 39 which says:

10-25

'(1)   Subject to this and any other Act, notwithstanding that the property in the goods may have passed to the buyer, the unpaid seller of goods, as such, has by implication of law -

(a) a lien on the goods or right to retain them for the price while he is in possession of them;

---

31 [1933] 2 All E.R. 370.

(b) in case of the insolvency of the buyer, a right of stopping the goods in transit after he has parted with the possession of them;

(c) a right of re-sale as limited by this Act.

(2)   Where the property in goods has not passed to the buyer, the unpaid seller has (in addition to his other remedies) a right of withholding delivery similar to and co-extensive with his rights of lien or retention and stoppage in transit where the property has passed to the buyer.'

It will be seen that, subject to the conditions set out in the other relevant sections, the seller has the possibility of exercising a lien on the goods, that is of retaining possession of them until he or she is paid, of reselling them or of stopping them in transit, that is by giving notice to the carrier not to deliver to an insolvent buyer.

INDEX